My Blood Divides and Unites

"Let's agree that the end goal is to have a non-racial world, with every-body co-existing peacefully. This book is a great guidepost."

– Tladi Ditshego, political exile, international affairs co-ordinator for Nelson Mandela during his tenure as ANC President, South Africa.

"Such a compelling, personal account of race and identity, and an important voice in our history and literature. Jesmane reflects on the past, brings us into the present and ushers us into a more hopeful future."

– Tumelo Marivate, Associate Director, Deloitte South Africa

MY BLOOD DIVIDES AND UNITES

Jesmane Boggenpoel

PORCUPINE PRESS

Johannesburg

First published in 2018 by
Porcupine Press
PO Box 2756
Pinegowrie, 2123
South Africa
admin@porcupinepress.co.za
www.porcupinepress.co.za

ISBN 978-1-928455-28-8

Designed and produced by Porcupine Press
Cover design: Charma Maluleka of Made2Fly

Set in 11 point on 15 point, Minion Pro

Printed and bound by Digital Action, Cape Town

Contents

To my parents, whose tremendous sacrificial love and support has made me all that I am.

To my mentor, the late Harvard Professor Calestous Juma. I truly appreciate his contribution to my life, and more broadly, to science, innovation and Africa.

Note to Readers

This book is written in American English, with limited exceptions, such as when using South African colloquialisms.

Although I use the words *race* and *racism* in this book, I understand that race is an artificial construct, often used by one race to oppress another.

Apartheid divided South Africans into four main racial groups: White, Indian, Coloured, and Black. For ease of explanation, I use this terminology in Chapters 1 through 4. In the remaining chapters, I use the term *Black* to collectively refer to all Africans, Coloureds, and Indians, in line with current legislation and practice in South Africa, with a few exceptions when specifically talking about the Coloured experience.

I capitalize the terms *White*, *Indian*, *Coloured*, and *Black* to highlight how much the apartheid regime obsessed over racial differences. Although I only speak of the Blacks, Coloureds, Indians, and Whites of South Africa, I understand that East Asians were also impacted by apartheid laws.

My narrative – and those of friends and associates – presents personal views and should not be ascribed to others or to groups of people, as the case may be.

In keeping with South African history and currently acceptable practice, I use the racial category *Coloured* throughout the book. Notwithstanding, I am aware of and sensitive to cultural differences in the United States, where this word is considered derogatory and offensive.

Introduction

I AM A proud and complete mixed-race woman whose genes represent a panoply of colors, of hues and shades, pastels and psychedelics, blended together to produce the beautiful mosaic of humanity that is me.

At least, that is how I see myself now. Growing up under apartheid I saw my heritage as "they" did, as an impenetrable brownish-blackish smudge of little note or worth.

Over time I came to realize that being of mixed race meant there was much beauty and value in my blood and in my past, an infinite variety of people and cultures, languages and customs, heroes and villains, oppressors and people who have been oppressed. I realized that my blood told the story of my past, of my nation's past, and in many respects, of humanity's past. I discovered that in my blood was the means to finally and truly understand who I was, to embrace all the people and peoples who are within me despite the innumerable conflicts and contradictions between them, and to draw tremendous hope and sustenance from doing so.

Most of all, I realized that my blood unites me so much more than it divides me, specifically because it chronicles my story.

We all have such a mosaic within, one that begins back in the mists of time and recounts our ancestral history as well as our personal story – and that story is continually added to as the days pass.

Apartheid threw a heavy curtain over my mosaic, shutting me off from my past. When apartheid fell I figuratively ripped the curtain away and studied my mosaic, eager to learn the story of my ancestry, of all that went into the making of me. What I initially saw was murky, for my mosaic had been crafted with the dim and few stones allowed to people of color until the fall of apartheid. Over time, with the help of genetic studies and travel to many different countries, I discovered that my genetic heritage is incredibly rich and that it contains more than a few, shall we say, contradictions. I am the product of newcomer and native, oppressor and oppressed, colonizer and colonized, slave master and slave. I am the product of the developed world and the developing world, White and Black, of German and Jew, of people who followed vastly different religions, and of many more groupings.

Uneasy about these contradictions, I was initially tempted to ignore the inconvenient truths in my story, to chisel them out of my mosaic so that I might focus on what it pleased me to know. But I realized that although I may not like certain pieces of my mosaic, they all contribute to the whole that is me. Plucking out offending pieces would leave blanks in my story and I would be telling a lie – to myself, and to others. I would essentially be rejecting myself.

This did not mean that I would have to hate a part of my past, and thus of myself. Instead, I could make it a point to learn as much about my past, about my identity, as possible, and embrace it all. I could accept the fact that some of my ancestors were oppressors who oppressed others of my ancestors. I could work to understand their points of view and, even when I disagreed or was disgusted, I could forgive them. The more I learnt of my past, and the more I reconciled the contradictions by forgiving and by embracing all the parts of my past and current stories, the more whole I felt. I am at peace with my past, with myself, and with my country.

Learning that I had to embrace the entirety of my story in order to accept and be true to myself was an important step forward in my personal healing. Until recently, I understood my world as being divided between oppressors and oppressed. Now I see that we are all the products of contradictions and unpleasant occurrences in our personal mosaics; that we are all the products of our pasts. It is the same for societies and countries, for they too have unhappy, shameful episodes and eras to contend with.

Rather than chisel these out of the story or gloss over them, it is vital that we learn what we can, accept and forgive, and work to see our mosaics in a new way. For me, this includes reinterpreting the story of oppression some of my ancestors suffered. For example, while my slave ancestors suffered, they also overcame. They demonstrated tremendous resilience, and today, the children of those slaves constitute a substantial portion of the South African population. They contributed significantly to the Afrikaans language. Indeed, some historians argue that slaves drove the development of the language as they attempted to communicate with slave owners, most of whom spoke Dutch. The slaves also had a major influence on South African cuisine, introducing new cooking methods and recipes such as curry, *bobotie*, and *koeksisters*. It is fair to say that parts of South Africa were built on the backs of the slaves, who labored to construct homes, farms, and buildings, many of which, including Cape Town's Castle of Good Hope, still stand.

I now see my slave ancestors as having been proud and resilient, suffering the worst the world could throw at them yet still maintaining their faith in themselves and in the future.

Today, I fully accept my past as it was and my ancestors as they were, knowing that lying beneath all the conflict is their human frailty, which includes their misdeeds and, for some, severe oppression of fellow humans. I accept the fact that some had different ethical and moral ideals than I do. I let go of my preconceived ideas and judgments of the past so that I may accept, forgive, and even try to love them as they are.

Looking to the future, I hold tightly to selected positive traits inherited from all my ancestors, free from the burden of having to reject or deny any of them. And in so doing, I am freed of the burden of having to reject or deny anyone today.

The process I struggled through – exploring my past so as to truly understand who I am, reconciling the various "parts" of me, and reframing my story in a new, more positive way – was difficult. It forced me to grapple with my pain, vulnerability, and other lingering emotions, and to reframe my story to one filled with hope. Doing so required that I forgive myself and others, even those I have viewed as oppressors. The process compelled me to tell my story, and to listen to the stories of others from around the world, including Nepal, India, Lebanon, Armenia, Rwanda and America. As I listened, I was introduced to different ways in which people have reconciled with their pasts and their oppressors, or have decided that this is simply too difficult to do. The process emphasized the need for me to bridge to others in order to develop authentic connections, even if we have stood on opposite sides of the line. It led me to explore the human fear of lack and desire to dominate, and possible solutions to overcome these. All this was vital to my healing and being set free.

The issues I grappled with are universal, which is why I believe the same process can be equally helpful to individuals, groups and nations as they struggle to build inclusive, harmonious, and prosperous futures for themselves and their constituent "parts." The process can be helpful for nations suffering from wounds as groups fight for control of the nation's narrative, resources, the reins of power, and more. These nations' futures will be determined by what happens now, so the "now" can be devoted to healing wounds and building an inclusive process. This, I firmly believe, requires that we work through the past to discover all the elements of identity, reconcile them in the present, reframe our stories, and become inspirational leaders for others so that all individuals and groups can look to the future, as one, with hope.

PART ONE

MY JOURNEY

I AM ... WHAT?

"White person" means a person who in appearance obviously is, or who is generally accepted as a white person, but does not include a person who, although in appearance obviously a white person, is generally accepted as a coloured person.
– South African Population Registration Act, 1951

APARTHEID WAS ALL about race, power, and wealth, about one race shaping the laws, economy, educational system, and other elements of society to ensure that they dominated all others. This was just and proper, they believed, for the "others" were naturally inferior. This was simply the ways things were, as they understood the world, and to arrange matters in any other way made no sense.

Many of the instruments of apartheid – such as the Group Areas Act and its effects on Blacks, Coloureds, and Indians[1] – are well known. Less noted are the ways in which apartheid deliberately enhanced racial and personal identity for some people while distorting and squashing it for others. This is because the makers of apartheid understood

---

1 During the apartheid regime, South Africans were, by law, divided into four primary groups: White, Indian, Coloured, and Black. The Whites, who were of European origin, were at the top of the hierarchy, maintaining strict political, economic, and social dominance over the other groups. Considerably below them were the Indians and the Coloureds (of mixed race). At the bottom of the hierarchy were the Blacks, who were descended from the indigenous inhabitants of the land. The Indians, Coloureds, and Blacks were all treated quite poorly: it was said that the Blacks were given one crumb that had fallen from the White tables, while the Indians and Coloureds were given two.

the power of identity, and they wanted to wield that power for their benefit. So did those who opposed apartheid, who sometimes strove to wield that same power against the hated regime.

For me, the issue of identity played out in very different ways.

I Will No Longer Be Defined by Apartheid

I always knew my ilk: Jesmane Boggenpoel, a Coloured girl growing up in Westbury, a Coloured township notorious for gangsterism and drugs. I went to Coloured elementary (primary) and high schools, most of my friends were Coloured, and I ate *bunnie chows, koeksisters*, and other foods enjoyed by the Coloured community. I found my community to be warm, fun, and lighthearted, though sometimes the lighthearted or teasing aspect could be taken too far, perhaps as a coping mechanism.

Coloured people originally arose in the former Cape of Good Hope,[2] out of a mixture of the indigenous Khoisan (Khoikhoi and San), European settlers, and slaves traded and imported from India, Indonesia, Sri Lanka, Madagascar, Mozambique, and other lands.[3]

I knew something of my ancestry: while both of my parents were Coloured, my mother's father was half Welsh and my mother's grandmother was half German and half St. Helene, which meant that

---

2 A portion of the area is currently in and around Cape Town, South Africa.

3 An infrastructure was developed at the Cape that included a fort and castle, jetties, a small town, and outlying farms. The aim was to provide fresh food and water, medical assistance, and repairs for the Dutch East India Company's ships involved in the spice trade in the East. This required a labor force able to carry out the back-breaking work needed to sustain such infrastructure in the harsh Cape environment. About 63,000 men, women, and children were shipped to the Cape as slaves between 1658 and the early 1800s, and many more were born into slavery at the Cape. "Many children were born in the Slave Lodge to slave couples, or to slave mothers with European fathers. Sailors and soldiers were allowed to 'visit' women in the Lodge in the evening. Many of these men treated the women as sex slaves, although a few formed relationships." Furthermore, there were sexual relationships between slave men and Khoisan women. Source: Slave Lodge museum, Cape Town.

one of her parents had come from St. Helena, the remote Atlantic Ocean island where the French Emperor Napoleon was imprisoned and died. I knew there was Irish lineage on my father's side and that his grandmother and sister had fair skin and red hair. There was also some Dutch thrown into the genetic mix from my father's side, plus a large dose of Indian – my mother's grandfather was from India.

I knew this about my personal ancestry, and I knew all about the Coloured community, its languages, religions, music, food, and more. Yet as I moved from my late teens into my early twenties, I wondered with increasing frequency and urgency, "Who am I?"

Later, as I began to travel to Europe in my mid-twenties, I met people not familiar with South African history who would ask me if I was of mixed race, inferring from my looks that one of my parents was Black and the other White. Was my mother Black and my father White, they would ask, or was it the other way around? They simply had no conception of what it meant to be Coloured, as defined by South African racial laws.

"Coloured" is an artificial concept created by the apartheid-era government to deal with the offspring of mixed marriages and mixed couplings, those "not-White, not-Black, not-Asian, not-nothing" children that resulted. Other than that, there was no reason for this group to exist. There was no ancestral land from which the Coloureds had come, nor was there a language of the Coloureds. We had no unique religious traditions, no mythology or philosophy, no ancient stories of derring-do, and no time of past greatness to recall with wistful fondness. Almost every element of culture we had was borrowed from others, with just a sprinkling of home-grown cultural elements such as the Coloured dialect and the music and dancing of the Cape Minstrels. We did not even have a unifying skin tone, for as a group, we sprawled across the spectrum with skin tone ranging from very dark to quite fair, hair ranging from kinky black to wavy brown to curly red and even some straight blonde, all within a single extended family. We had very little of the stuff of common culture, yet there we were, lumped together by law, seen and treated as one by the others. They weren't quite sure what to make of us and forced us to attempt to make something out of this concoction.

Were we really Black, if imperfectly so? After all, commencing in the mid-1600s, it was sexual congress between natives and newcomers (European settlers, imported slaves) that produced "not-Black, not-White" children, and recent mitochondrial DNA studies, which trace ancestry through the maternal line, show that we are largely descended from the Khoisan, the oldest indigenous inhabitants of Southern Africa, whose presence in the area can be dated back 140,000 years. And our love of dance, celebration, and spirit of community and sharing was inherited from our Black ancestors.

Were we really White, if imperfectly so? After all, the Coloureds generally spoke Afrikaans and English, which are the languages of the Whites. Our Christian religion was very Anglo-Saxon, as were our favorite sports. Even our standard of "beauty" was decidedly more White than Black, with light skin, straight hair, and "sharp features" (a White-looking nose) being preferred.

Or were we really something else entirely, neither "not-quite-Black" nor "not-quite-White" but truly Coloured? After all, these same genetic studies have demonstrated that of all the people on the planet, our DNA is the most varied, which means that as a group we are truly not like any others.

But are we really a group? And if so, what makes us so, other than law? I never thought of these things when I was young, although when hanging out with Black friends, I sometimes thought it would be nice if I was more Black, while I sometimes wished I could be more White when hanging out with White friends. Like almost all Coloured families, mine had bare branches on the family tree, gaps in our knowledge caused by the fact that the identity of the father, or one or both of the grandfathers, was often unknown. For us, the missing piece was my father's father, whom few family members other than my grandmother had ever met, and they guarded the secret of his identity. This didn't trouble me when I was young, for it was so common. Remember, we were often seen as the embarrassing leftovers, generally the result of intimacy between a woman of color and a White man who might wish to forget or that his family might force him to hide. Family history was not discussed much; we largely accepted the assertion that we were Coloured and did not pierce the veil.

This was not really an issue from the time these unions began in the mid-1600s, for during those years, the mixed-race children produced were absorbed into either White society[4] or slave or Khoisan society. From the early 1800s, the mixed-race population – incorporating slaves, former slaves who had gained their freedom, and later the Khoisan – informally coalesced. Yet, Coloureds were still a malleable and loose community living in harmony with other races, with individuals from other races assimilated into its community and vice versa. Yes, the pre-apartheid government had enacted laws to restrict Coloured opportunities, but there was not yet a sense of our being a strictly boundaried group.

Then came the moment of authoritarian creation in the 1950s, when bureaucrats carefully selecting their words fashioned the Coloured legal category by lumping together those who were neither White nor Black in appearance[5] – or who *might* have been White or Black in appearance but who were not generally accepted as either White or Black. Quickly realizing that this clumsy definition was inadequate, the bureaucrats bolstered it with various practical assessments such as the "pencil test," which consisted of pushing a pencil into a person's hair and seeing what happened. If the pencil fell to the floor the person "passed" the test and was considered to be White, but if the pencil remained in place, the hair was judged kinky and the person Coloured.

Not only was the Coloured community separated by apartheid fiat, it was locked in place by laws prohibiting marriage or extramarital sexual activity between Coloureds and any others. Earlier laws had

---

4 European men could marry slave women only after they attained their free status and had a Christian baptism. These women and their offspring were assimilated into White society. Children conceived in extramarital, mixed unions and their mothers were more likely not assimilated into White society. If the child's mother was a slave, the child likewise had a slave life. Source: Cape Melting Pot, translated into English in 2000 by Delia Robertson from HF Heese's 1985 book Groep Sonder Grense.

5 Over the next two decades the racial classification of Coloured was extended into the following racial groups: Cape Coloured, Malay, Griqua and "Other Coloured".

prohibited such activity between Whites and people of color, but apartheid prohibited it across *any* racial lines – between Coloureds and Blacks, Coloureds and Indians, and Coloureds and Whites.

Although never put to the test, I was clearly Coloured, and in my late teens and early twenties began to wonder what that meant. While I dearly loved and appreciated my family and community, when looking back into our history, I could not help but see the shame of being an illegitimate group and not truly knowing who we were – the narrative crafted for us by apartheid. Most of all, I felt a void. Although I had been taught in school about the intrepid Dutch and British explorers, the Boer trekkers, Shaka Zulu, and other historical figures, there was hardly any discussion of Coloured history in our textbooks. The Whites in South Africa could trace their roots back to the Dutch and English; the Blacks to their various tribal histories, cultures, and traditions that run too far back in history to measure; the Indians to their ancestral subcontinent from which sprang numerous storied cultures and kings, philosophies, religions, and literature. But the Coloureds? Collectively, we could point back no further than the mid-1600s, when the first wave of mixed children was produced, some as the result of long-lasting love, some from a brief moment of lust, and some of rape. Individually, I could not go even that far, for I could not climb very high up my family tree. Remember, as the "leftovers" group, we were often cut off from our recent ancestors, and when those individual connections were cut, so were the cultural ties. Although I knew my great-grandfather was Welsh, for example, I had no feeling of being Welsh. No Welsh traditions or words or foods had been passed down to me and my siblings, we heard no stories of the old days in Wales, and we had no Welsh knickknacks on our shelves. It was the same with respect to my Khoisan and Irish heritage: those were simply things I knew as abstract facts, but from which I drew no sense of direct cultural heritage. The nearest thing to cultural heritage my family had was the "Indian porridge" called *soji* we ate and the *biryani* we enjoyed at Christmas, two practices passed down from my mother's grandfather from India.

All I knew for sure was that I was a Coloured girl growing up in a Coloured community, going to Coloured schools, and eating foods enjoyed by the Coloured community. For some, this was enough. For me, it was not. Knowing your heritage generates pride; knowledge of your family history, its stories and personalities, and its accomplishments and failures gives you a sense of who you are. I had no such knowledge, no ancestral pride, and never fully accepted myself, for it is hard to accept yourself in the face of unknowns. I felt my true heritage – whatever it might be – had been snatched away, and I had been forced to choose whether I would be either "not-quite-White" or "not-quite-Black." For many Coloureds in the apartheid era, the choice was easy: lean toward White because if you could "play White," that is, pass as White, you could get a better job, live in a better neighborhood, go to a White hospital when you were ill, and otherwise benefit. Once apartheid was swept away there was a tug in the opposite direction, for being viewed as Black might open the door to certain privileges.

For me, this jockeying for position made matters worse. I didn't want to pick and choose from the strands of my heritage to gain a legal or economic advantage. I wanted to embrace all the strands, to draw strength and wisdom and humor from all of them. But apartheid said, "No, you are Coloured, you cannot claim the native Khoikhoi, Welsh, Dutch, Indian, or other strands on your family tree. You may only claim the Coloured strand, the one invented by the bureaucrats. You are not permitted to feel pride in your heritage, for you have none. You are Coloured, and Coloureds are a bit of an embarrassment." This was my narrative, dictated by apartheid, and it bred shame and rejection.

Upon graduating from a Coloured high school in 1990, I looked forward to attending the University of the Witwatersrand in Johannesburg. "Wits," as we called it, was a mixed, liberal university, but when I arrived, I was terribly disappointed to find very few Coloured students. I felt envious of other race groups who could cling to each other in their own cliques. Unable to cling to my own, I was forced to make friends with everyone: Blacks, Indians, and Whites. I met wonderful people who have remained close friends since. I broadened my horizons but did not develop a keener sense of what it meant to be Coloured and felt even more cut off from my roots, such as they were.

Only about 10 percent of the South African population is Coloured, and only a tiny percentage of us had the qualifications to be accountants, so as I moved into the business world, I found myself increasingly alone, so to speak, and began to identify more and more with the Black strands of my heritage.

This is how the matter rested until I was in my mid-thirties, and my brother began to ask our mother questions about our family. She could not answer them any better now than she could when we were young, and the Coloured attitude toward delicate questions about family remained the same: don't ask. Burning with curiosity, I sat down one night, did some back-of-the-envelope calculations, and developed an Excel spreadsheet showing what percentage of our blood – mine and my siblings' – was Black and European and Indian and everything else. This was non-scientific evidence, for we had only family lore to rely on and that was incomplete at best. Yet there it was for the first time in my life and any of our lives: our heritage expressed as percentages of this and that race. There were no stories, pictures, or personalities to bring it alive, no new facts or insights, just what we already knew presented in mathematical terms. Yet, somehow, it was amazing. It felt as if we were connected to a past – to *our* past.

And that was how the matter rested for another eight years until early 2016 when a friend told me in Davos that he had recently had his DNA tested through a company called 23andMe and suggested I do the same. Intrigued, I ordered the kit online and waited for it to arrive, delighted that it appeared so quickly via express mail. I spat into the tube, sealed it in an envelope, and mailed it back to New York. About eleven weeks later, I received the results and was very surprised to find out that I wasn't just *somewhat* Welsh and *somewhat* German. Instead, I was 38.4 percent European with a rather large dollop (6.2 percent) of Ashkenazi Jewish. My genetic heritage was 28.6 percent Sub-Saharan African, while a quarter was South Asian (Indian) and 6.9 percent East Asian.[6] Within my East Asian heritage is some Chinese descent,

---

6 The remaining 1 percent of my genetic heritage was unassigned by 23andMe.

from my father's lineage, with his paternal haplogroup[7] being Han Chinese.

These may seem like random numbers to you, but to me, my brother, and my parents, they were a treasure! Suddenly, I felt more connected to myself and to the world around me. I felt a sense of wholeness and was more at peace than ever because I finally knew what my makeup was. It was only numerical knowledge bereft of stories, personalities, and pictures, but to me, it was very meaningful.

I have an American friend, a Jewish man, who didn't understand my fascination with these results. When I told him that learning this brought me to tears, he was puzzled. "What's so emotionally powerful about being 38.4 percent European and 28.6 percent Sub-Saharan African?" he asked. "Suppose it had been reversed and you were 38.4 percent Sub-Saharan African and 28.6 percent European? Would that make you feel different?"

"No," I replied, "it would be just as wonderful."

My friend has a rich cultural heritage, which he figuratively traces back to George Washington *and* Moses, to the U.S. Constitution *and* the Ten Commandments, to incredibly long lists of American, Jewish, and American-Jewish authors, scientists, poets, athletes, philosophers, movie stars, and much more. "You have so much heritage," I explained to him, "that you have no idea what it means to have so little. And now I have some more."

Certainly, not all Coloured people would agree with me. Many are happily connected to what they find to be a rich and deeply satisfying culture. And with apartheid and its disingenuous directives on identity gone, the Coloured community is free to develop in an organic way. In the not-too-distant future, there may be a deeply rich and vibrant Coloured narrative, history, and culture that is distinct from the others and that draws on its own sources of strength and inspiration.

In the meantime, these results have allowed me to reframe my narrative, to kick aside the apartheid-imposed tale of nothingness and

---

7 The Y chromosome carried only by males and passed down from father to son in every generation.

shame, and to replace it with a rich heritage. My personal narrative is now filled with pride, for I feel connected to peoples, societies, customs, and cultures from all over the world. My career and love for exotic sojourns take me to many places on different continents, and wherever I travel, whoever I meet, I feel a kinship. No one is the "other" for me, for I am the product of many peoples and many societies; I am the offspring of them all. Almost everywhere I go, I feel as if one of my ancestors was there, perhaps speaking this language, eating these foods, or singing this music – and it's all in me. The world is in my blood.

I'm continuing to explore my past. Regarding my Khoisan lineage, I've visited the caves where the San had lived at least ten thousand years ago in the Cradle of Humankind (on the outskirts of Johannesburg), which gave me a special connection to my tribal ancestors and their ancient home.

In addition to the Khoisan of Southern Africa, my African ancestry takes me back to Somalia, Senegal, the Mende from Sierra Leone, the Mbuti and Bayaka from the Congo, the Maasai of Kenya, the Yoruba of Nigeria, and Akan from Ghana and Côte d'Ivoire. Now, I truly feel I am African, with the blood of many peoples all across the African continent flowing through me.

Further away, I also learned that my German blood dates back to somewhere between the time Mozart and Beethoven were born in the mid-1700s and the German Revolutions of 1848, which nearly toppled counts and kings. Could this mean that one of my ancestors enjoyed a live concert from either of these musical geniuses – or perhaps commissioned one of their masterpieces? What we know from family lore is that a German soldier with the family name Fritz was injured in battle, went to a hospital for treatment, and wound up falling in love with and marrying his nurse, a woman from the island of St. Helena. In which of many possible battles was he injured? On which side did he fight? Was he a valued officer or cannon fodder? The newlyweds lived in St. Helena and then in the small town of Colesberg in South Africa, where they bought and worked a sheep farm. That's where their known story ends; that's all we know about my great-great-grandparents.

I traveled to Wales, the birthplace of Arthur Collins, my mother's father's father, who was the only one of my great-grandparents I ever met, albeit briefly. While in Wales, I toured Cardiff Castle and walked through the adjacent park grounds. Great-grandfather fought in World War I, and while there, I learned that the Welsh soldiers were trained at or near the very castle where I was standing! Was I in a courtyard where he had once stood at rigid attention while receiving orders from an officer? Was I strolling through the park where he once pitched his tent, pumped out pushups, or played cricket with his buddies? I may never know, but simply being where he probably was; seeing the sun, sky, and River Taff as he had; and breathing the same air and napping under the same trees he had suddenly made him feel very much alive to me.

Sometimes my head fills with fantasies about my named and many unnamed ancestors who have suddenly appeared on my family tree. Are any of these fancies true? Who knows? But I can dream. And since I've deduced that my Ashkenazi Jewish roots trace back to Hungary and Romania, I travelled to those countries where I felt a connection to my ancestors. Also on my travel radar are Congo, Somalia, and Sierra Leone to explore my African lineage, Tamil Nadu and Gujarat in India, and Indonesia. Yes, I have but intangible genetic links to these countries and to other countries and groups I've mentioned. But to me, they are as powerful as an entire gallery of paintings of ancestor after ancestor, and even more real. I feel as if I truly have an identity, and I am in part defined by that identity rather than by apartheid.

It Is Possible to Define Your Own Identity
As I've shared these stories and spoken about identity with friends and others, I've discovered that there are many ways of understanding and constructing one's identity. My American friend, Ian Solomon, a conflict-management expert, has an intriguing way of looking at this idea. He also has an intriguing heritage as the son of a Jewish-American mother and a Black-American father, raised by his mother and Jewish-American stepfather, with two adopted Native American siblings.

"Identity is not fixed," Ian says. "It's a dialectic between personal and social construction. What do you see yourself as, and what does the world allow you to see yourself as? Identity is fluid," he continues, "evolving as society evolves and from society to society. It can be a source of pride and joy or of pain, something to embrace or to reject and bury. We are all complex tapestries, woven and rewoven throughout life. Some of our threads, like race, are fixed, and sometimes these are the only threads that matter, as was the case in South Africa during apartheid. But many threads are not fixed, which means we can decide which are important to us, and how to weave our identity tapestry."

Apartheid-era South Africa refused to allow people to craft their own tapestries. Instead, the government proclaimed that some people were this while others were that, with no exceptions possible. Making matters worse, members of certain groups were strongly pressured to adopt "approved" thoughts and attitudes, no matter how poor a fit these might be. Today, with the fall of apartheid two decades in the past, I wonder how many people still feel they must think and act in line with the past.

Opening the Doors of Perception

In many cases, it is difficult to realize that your perception of reality and identity is influenced by the lingering effects of apartheid – or other forms of bigotry and hatred – because you are caught up in the world it has created. Yes, that world is artificial, but since it is all you know, it can be difficult to realize there is anything different. My brother Kent is ten years younger than me, which means he was only ten when apartheid fell. Still, it only took those few years to warp the way he saw himself and others. Here's how he describes it:

> *Thinking of identity was a subconscious process, for being Coloured isn't connected to physical appearance: some of my relatives look White, some look mixed, and some look more Indian. We have this strong label of being Coloured, but it's just a story. The Coloured community isn't homogeneous; there are Christians and Muslims, and while we are a fusion of African, Asian, and European ancestry, each Coloured family has*

completely unique percentages and mixtures due to their unique family history. It's really just the story that connects us, and the story is that there are separate races and a scale of superiority with the Whites on top, Blacks on the bottom, and Indians and Coloureds in the middle. But when you leave the country the story falls apart, for people outside South Africa don't know that story. It's the "reality" in South Africa, but not elsewhere.

The story had, and still has, power in South Africa. After apartheid, very shortly post-1994, my mother took me out of the Coloured elementary school. She wanted me to have access to a better education, so she placed me in a previously government White-only school, what they called a Model C school at the time. There were a few Coloured kids, barely any Black kids, and the rest were White. Up until then, I hadn't mixed much with others outside of our community, but then it was blatant: "I'm Coloured, they're not, and there's something separating us." My closest friends in the school were Coloured. We did have friendships across the group lines, but not deep friendships.

It seemed like there was an invisible wall between us, and this wall was created by our conditioning. The White kids had been conditioned to think, "This is outside our comfort zone," and we Coloured kids were used to interacting only with other Coloureds. It was subconscious programming that remained in the South African mental landscape and in the minds of people of all groups, even after the fall of apartheid. The programming – the conditioning – remains, although it's slowly starting to change. Today, people of all groups work together in the workplace but don't develop the deep relationships that you see in other places in the world where there aren't these deep racial divides. It's not conscious; you don't think, "I can't have White friends" or "I can't have Black friends." You're friendly and interact with others, but your subconscious conditioning tells you that you can only develop really deep friendships with people of the same racial group.

It is hard to break this programming; it's the wizard behind the curtain. We didn't speak about it and didn't follow it consciously, but it directed our reality. For me, traveling was important, for it got me to question my perception of reality, of self, and of others. It got me to question the conditioning that told me that other races of humans were less than or more than me. I needed distance from the country; I needed to get away from the programming in order to question the programming.

Soon after completing a Bachelor of Science degree in Information Technology, I moved to Japan for two years teaching English on the JET (Japan Exchange and Teaching) Program in order to gain some living abroad experience. While doing so, I found out that the mindscapes of others outside of the country were vastly different to that of South Africans, and yet the humanity of our condition and existence was the same all over the world. Over the years I lived amongst Japanese, Koreans, Indians, Indonesians, and Peruvians and met people of all races, nationalities, religions, languages and cultures, from all over the world. All the travel and living abroad helped liberate me from the apartheid narrative. The narrative didn't stand up to my life experiences when I traveled – it couldn't, because it's such a distorted picture of reality. It <u>had</u> to fall apart once I was away from South Africa and began forming deep relationships with people of all backgrounds.

We can only liberate our consciousness through deep introspection and questioning of the mind realities that have formed the basis of who we are. It's not necessary to leave the country you are from to free your mind, but it helps you understand and deeply question your programming and mindscape by going far outside of yourself and the "reality" that you happened to be born into.

Identity Influences Destiny

I feel that identity is a very personal matter influencing every aspect of a person's life, from dress to speech, from feelings about yourself today to your hopes or fears for the future. Identity goes a long way toward determining whether you believe it is possible to improve your condition, to work with others for mutual benefit, and even to build a nation.

That is why I feel it is vital that everyone work out their own sense of identity, that they feel free to do so and are accorded respect, whether or not others hold different views. Doing so requires time and reflection, especially when oppressive external forces are trying to bend your identity to their needs. However, the time and effort invested in identity creation are well worth it, for the very act of crafting an identity is healing, liberating, and strengthening. Since identity is dynamic, the process is often on-going. Rather than viewing this process as a never-ending chore, I see it as an opportunity to find more healing and liberation and to evermore develop strength and resilience.

CHOICES & WALLS

GROWING UP, I pretty much remained within the physical bounds of the Coloured community. Apartheid was always present but in the background, so to speak, and did not require me to make daily choices. Much more immediate were my neighborhood and family, and these were as different as day and night. In a sense, the neighborhood represented the choices made on my behalf by apartheid, choices driven by disdain and disgust, greed and fear on the part of others. My family, however, represented all the loving and hopeful choices that had been made for me.

Literally standing between neighborhood and family was the wall my grandfather built at our house in Westbury, and it was both a physical and a symbolic separation. As a kid, while I thought it was sweet that my dear Grampa built us a wall, I never gave much thought to it. I'm looking at a picture of the wall as I write this, taken when my twin sister, Julie-Ann, and I were about sixteen years old, and our brother was six. It's one of those shots you'll find in every family album, showing the kids standing together outside the house, the older ones smiling and at ease, the young one more playful. In our case, he's flashing the peace sign with both hands, and his sports cap is on backwards.

The wall, made of bricks, is about five feet (one and a half meters) tall and coated with a dimply-looking plaster that gives it texture. On top, Grampa placed a series of wider bricks that cap the whole thing off, and he used plaster to create a series of little lumps on these capstones. The lumps, which are irregularly shaped and spaced, cast tiny shadows that move about the capstones as the sun moves across the sky. When Grampa was finished building the wall, Daddy painted it cream.

It's a nice wall, though probably not terribly remarkable as walls go. It was, however, quite a remarkable thing to see in Westbury, where only a handful of houses had such a wall. Remember, Westbury was one of those townships built on the outskirts of Johannesburg, filled with small houses thrown up overnight, cramped, and constructed of a brick called ash brick, which was inferior but good enough for Coloureds. Like the others, our house had a living room, kitchen, three small bedrooms, and one bathroom. It was "just enough," as we said, but nothing more than that.

Neither was the neighborhood anything to brag about, as it lacked grocery stores, parks, restaurants, and almost everything else you associate with a family neighborhood. There were some little stores called "tuck shops," which were informal shops set up inside people's houses. The family would set aside a little portion of one room in the house and stock some milk, bread, crisps, and other small items. It was our version of 7-Eleven, although a typical tuck shop might only have twenty different items for sale. I used to love to buy "fluffy puffs," crispy little sticks made of corn and dusted with cheese.

The one thing we had in abundance was gangs: Westbury was notorious for its gangsterism, with small groups of youths hanging out on street corners. The neighborhood had an odd relationship with the gangs, for while they were against us in the sense that they trafficked in theft, drugs, rape, and who knows what else, they were accepted as the way things were. All those young men hanging around, looking for opportunities to snatch something, maybe rape or shoot someone, were our friends' brothers and cousins. You certainly never dared challenge the gangs, for they would react violently. As for calling the police when they got out of hand, that was an exercise in futility. You might as well talk to our wall.

We feared the gangs, but we learned to live with them. Women respectfully returned their "greetings," which sounded like a cricket chirping – "*sk skkk*" – and was a less-than-gentlemanly salutation. Either that, or they would say, "Hello, *meisie*" (*meisie* is Afrikaans for "girl").

One day, I was walking from our house to the place where you catch the local informal taxis or mini vans, on my way to the Highgate Mall. I usually treated the gangsters very carefully but that day just wasn't up to responding to the *"sk skkk"* that greeted me as I passed a gangster.

That was a bad idea, for the gangster who had chirped out the greeting immediately hurried to catch me, grabbed my arm, and said in a rough and menacing way, "Why don't you greet me? I know your face and what route you take. Next time you come this way, you know what I'll do to you."

To me, that could only mean rape. For a moment I froze; I just stood there, stupefied. Then, I quickly broke away and jumped into a taxi. For the next several months, every time I passed that corner, I looked around nervously, wondering if he was waiting for me. Maybe he had seen me coming and was lurking nearby, ready to make good his threat. Fortunately, I never saw him again.

Westbury was reserved for Coloureds, which meant that Whites did not purchase homes there, and it was quite unusual to see one walking down the street. It was not so rare, however, to see a White man arrive in a car or on a motorcycle, park in front of certain homes, go in for just a little while, then return to his vehicle and drive away. These homes were drug houses. I knew that by the time I was six or seven and used to pass by several drug houses every morning on my daily forty-minute walk to school, then again on the way home.

Fortunately, the drug houses weren't much of a day-to-day problem for us, as long as we steered clear of them. Neither were the visiting Whites an issue, for they came and went quickly. There's only one time I know of that a White caused a problem. It happened at the house of a friend of mine. One afternoon, a White man knocked on their door and asked to use their bathroom – a bit ironic, considering that Coloureds weren't allowed to use White bathrooms! My friend's parents said yes, and the White man went into their bathroom, locking the door behind him. The parents heard the door lock, then all was silent for a very long time. Finally, the parents knocked gently on the door, thinking their visitor might be ill. They knocked, waited, knocked, waited, and knocked some more, louder and more urgently. Finally, after much knocking, worrying, and waiting, they called the police, who would come because a White was involved. Paramedics arrived, forced their way into the bathroom, and discovered the White man on the floor, unconscious. He had injected himself with some drugs. They quickly gave him emergency medications that revived him, and shortly after he regained consciousness he surprised everyone by running off!

I've thought back on these things and upon life in general in Westbury many times since becoming an adult, and the more I think about them, the more impressive my grandfather's wall seems to me. In a physical sense, it's just bricks and plaster, but in my mind, it represents all the wonderful things that my family was to me.

Most obviously, the wall was security. Grampa wanted to protect us from the sometimes-deadly violence in the street. But it was more than that, for a plain brick wall would have served. Grampa spent a great deal of extra time and expended more effort than necessary to make that wall as beautiful as possible, even creating those little plaster lumps along the top, the ones that make the wall look just a little bit different at different times of the day as they caught the sun and cast their little shadows. I suppose Grampa was, in his way, trying to compensate for the ill fate that had befallen our family. Apartheid ensured that the Coloureds, as a group, were very poor, and it was not unusual for the man of the family to be forced to travel long distances to find decent work. My father, who was skilled in construction carpentry, had to travel by train to work. When I was two, he suffered a nervous breakdown while on a train returning home from an exhausting, abusive work contract. My mother, who had not completed high school, was forced to become the main provider for our family in an era when there were almost no opportunities for women, let alone all Coloured people. As a result, we were very poor, even for Coloureds.

Although Grampa's wall couldn't protect us from the ills of apartheid and poverty, it was strong and beautiful enough to create an inner space where the love and support of family was showered upon us. Within the confines of the wall, there was always affection and hope.

I wish I had some grand story of family love to write about here, one filled with drama, danger, and with an Oscar-worthy resolution. But that's not the way family love plays out, at least not in our case. Instead, there were a thousand and one instances, though small or even trivial on their own. There was, for example, the time when Julie-Ann and I were six years old, and Mummy walked us the forty minutes to school. We were among the many "walking poor," those without funds to buy a car. It was raining that day and we arrived quite wet, so Mummy walked back home, got two sets of dry clothing, returned to school, and helped us change. Then, Mummy walked back home for the second time in the rain. "She must really love you to do this," our teacher said to us.

Bullying was common at school, I was often a target because I was very skinny, unusually so in a community where a "Jennifer Lopez-type" body was both more common and preferred. It didn't help that English was my mother tongue in a community where most spoke Afrikaans. English was considered to be a "weaker" language, making me an easier target. Nasty classmates would constantly jab a sharpened pencil into my arm and, several times, I was threatened with a *fego*, which is slang for a physical fight. I was scared to death by these threats, for being so skinny, I was sure I would be beaten badly. Fortunately, these threats of a fego were just that: threats. Mummy went to my school, spoke to the teacher, and made sure the threats stopped. She also told me that the other kids picked on me because they were jealous of the smart girl, turning me into the hero of the story rather than the victim.

As I grew older, I began to understand how many sacrifices our parents made on our behalf. Even the fact that my mother stayed with our father after his breakdown and again after his relapse was an expression of her love. She could have strayed and gone off with other men, but she stayed with us during ten long, difficult years. When my sister and I were young, mummy would bring home books she purchased at a discount from the bookstore where she worked – she wanted us to read as much as possible and instilled in us a love for reading. As we grew older, she continually reminded us of the importance of education and that no matter how anyone else viewed us, in her eyes we were special and well able to accomplish anything we set out to do.

Then there was Uncle Reg Luckay, who encouraged my parents to transfer my sister and me from our local Coloured high school to a better one further away from our house that offered the "higher-grade" math and science courses necessary to get into science and commerce (finance) departments at university. This was very important for us, as my sister and I had decided at an early age that she wanted to become a medical doctor and I a chartered accountant.[8] A high school generally only offered good quality, higher-grade courses if it had a sufficient number of students who had done well enough to qualify for the advanced coursework, and our local high school had only a handful of such students. That's why Uncle Reg urged us to transfer to Chris J. Botha Senior Secondary School in Bosmont, where he taught math. He lived nearby the school and once a week, when school was over, would drive Julie-Ann and me to his house for math tutoring. We were joined there by our second cousin, Karen, and her friend.

We would sit together in his living room and spend two hours working through the advanced math problems we had to master to be admitted to university. Uncle Reg would begin by introducing the concept for the day, then give us a set of problems he had prepared for us to work through. We would do so individually in our notebooks before reviewing our work together. We wanted this extra tutoring because we had our hearts set on going to university; and we also enjoyed it because Uncle Reg was so patient and kind. He had ways of explaining concepts so that they seemed simple and was willing to go over and over everything until we all understood it.

I could relate many more instances of family love, many more times and ways in which my parents and others helped us thrive in the face of adversity. But I think you get the point. You understand how much they loved us and were willing to sacrifice on our behalf. That was their choice, a powerful and positive choice that pushed back against the negative choices heaped on us by apartheid.

---

8 A Chartered Accountant is equivalent to the Certified Public Accountant (CPA) in the U.S. In South Africa, many business leaders have the Chartered Accountant qualification.

Many of my peers lacked the figurative wall that is a strong family to buffer them from the cruel effects of apartheid. It was not at all uncommon for girls to become pregnant and drop out of high school, for the boys to become involved with gangs and steal car rims, and for both girls and boys to drop out of school because they were distracted and seduced by other things. It was not uncommon for youngsters to make choices or be forced into choices that foreclosed rather than opened new and positive possibilities in their lives. This was not always due to a lack of family love and support, yet having these things made it much easier to deal with the "world beyond the wall."

Wall of Faith

Standing outside of our house, you could easily see Grampa's wall. If you came inside, you would quickly sense the presence of another wall, a "wall of faith" that was as powerful and protective as the physical wall outside. I was certainly aware of the presence and strength of faith early in life, for it came beaming forth from Granny.

Granny, Grampa's wife, was a Coloured woman named Lilian with an identical twin sister named Iris. Granny gave birth to identical twin daughters, my mother and her sister Naomi, and my mother gave birth to identical twin daughters of her own.

Granny became deeply spiritual and studied at the Johannesburg Bible College for a year in her early forties. But then she developed pink eye, and two botched surgeries performed at a substandard hospital left her blind. A White woman from the blind school in Newclare came to the house every week to teach Granny how to read braille, and from then until the end of her life, she daily ran her fingers lightly over the words in her special Bible, drawing inspiration from the passages she read over and over.

Eventually, Granny had to drop her Bible studies. Never one to let problems stand in her way, she became our "family pastor." We, her family, were her "flock of sheep," and she constantly prayed for and guided us. She prayed for my physical aprotection, and she prayed that I might do well at school. Whenever I was discouraged, she would remind me of the 37th Psalm: "Delight yourself in the Lord, and He will give you the desires of your heart." Whenever I was afraid of failing or of anything else, she would urge me on by quoting from the 27th Psalm: "The Lord is my light and my salvation – whom shall I fear?" She passed away many years ago, but I have an indelible memory of her sitting in our lounge, which doubled as the dining room, reading her braille Bible and looking up and smiling when she heard someone approaching, ready with encouragement, always urging us to stand tall in the face of adversity, and enveloping us in her faith, which became our faith.

Granny passed her faith on to her children, including Mummy. My mother believed that God had blessed her, despite the difficult circumstances of her life; from the time she was a child, she felt the presence of the Holy Spirit in her life showing her right from wrong and leading her in the right direction.

The presence of the Holy Spirit was strong when my father became ill and was sent to the mental institution Fort Beaufort for treatment. This hospital was far away, and Mummy could not go visit him or receive any information whatsoever from other family members or the doctors. For months, there was nothing but silence, and in that silence, Mummy heard the voice of the Holy Spirit telling her that not only would Daddy recover, he would also be released in time for Easter. And he was. Everyone else in the family, along with our friends, was sure Daddy would not come out of the hospital at all, for few patients did. Only Mummy had faith, and her faith was rewarded.

The presence of the Holy Spirit was particularly powerful when my little sister Corinne was born and died. In Mummy's words:

> *When my little Corinne was born in 1982, she cried so very softly that I knew something was wrong. Although I came through the delivery well, I could see that the doctors were worried, and Corinne was quickly taken away for treatment. Later that day, my doctor came to my room to tell me that Corinne was not going to make it. I went to see her and was surprised at how beautiful she looked – yet, she was dying. I only saw her for five minutes lying in her special crib with IV and oxygen tubes attached to her. It was all I could take at the time.*

The very next day, the nurse came to my room to tell me that Corinne had passed away. I went numb; it hurt so much that I went completely numb and remained that way. I wondered how it would be possible to ever feel anything again.

Later that day, as I was lying very still and quiet on my bed, I suddenly saw a bright light on the left corner of the bed. Then, all at once, God appeared in that spot, sitting on the bed, clothed in a white robe and stretching His hands out to me. Even as His hands reached out to me, they seemed to cast forth a sense of peace that enveloped me and has remained with me since.

I believe that God came to me in my sorrow and that His presence carried me through the difficult days of grieving. He was so real, so comforting – I will never forget what He did for me at that moment.

Granny and Mummy passed their faith on to me. From as early as I can remember, the family regularly attended church. Until I left for university, Grampa, Granny, my parents, siblings, and I would go together each Sunday morning. During the services, the pastor would talk about how a particular Bible teaching related to something happening in his own life or that of the community, and explain how we could apply the lesson of this passage to our lives. I listened fairly closely, and one lesson I embraced early in life was that God loved me just as I was and would enable me.

I continued attending church as well as praying once I went off to university. My sister and I met often on campus and at home. We would talk about life, about our successes and failures, hopes and fears, and pray for each other. I remember feeling the presence of God so strongly when praying for Julie-Ann. This is a very difficult thing to define, for it wasn't something to be seen or heard. Instead, it was a powerful feeling that the divine presence is with you, within you, bringing with Him a powerful feeling of peace and harmony, a sense that there *is* purpose to your life and the lives of others, as well as hope for overcoming struggles. He is always ready to guide you and your loved ones forward, and He will offer you His grace.

Whether we are two inches or an ocean and a continent apart, we still support and feel sustained by each other in prayer.

"Filling the Gaps"

Apartheid made choices for me, choices that constricted life for Coloureds and "others" like me. Among these were the series of regulations that consigned Coloureds to a lesser education, a narrower range of job opportunities, and lower salaries for work performed, compared to Whites. This meant that I, like so many others, did not receive nearly the elementary and secondary education I should have and that my family, like so many others, was poorer than it should have been.

I didn't think about this when I was young, for it was simply the way things were. But when I went off to university and realized how many more educational opportunities the White students had, I began to worry. I had been a top high school student, but that was in the inferior Coloured school system. We did not have the computer lab, biology lab, and other educational aids, the cricket field, swimming pool, and other recreational facilities, or the wide breadth of subjects offered in White schools and private schools. We had, on average, ten to twenty more students per class than did the White schools.

Now at Wits University, I realized that it was not only educational opportunities I had been denied: there were numerous other "gaps in my wall" that needed to be filled. Many of these related to practical, mundane areas of life that others took for granted. Each on its own was a manageable problem, but collectively, they were taxing. One of these challenges was driving. Back then, you were eligible to take the test for a learner's permit at age seventeen and the driving test a year later. But this assumed that your family owned a car and would teach you how to drive or that they had enough money to pay for private lessons. Neither was true in my case, for as I mentioned earlier, we were of the "walking poor" who could not afford a car. We walked almost everywhere, even to the doctor when we were sick, if a car-owning relative was not available. Bus service to our neighborhood was spotty, and formal taxis were expensive for us – even Whites used them sparingly.

My inability to drive wasn't a problem when I lived on the Wits campus, since I could walk from my dormitory to the classrooms and other places I needed to go. However, when I wanted to return to my family home in Westbury – which I did almost every weekend – I had to take public transportation. The commute home began with a thirty-five-to-forty-minute walk from campus to the "taxi rank," where the unlicensed minivans that hired out as taxis would congregate. This walk took me through some not-very-nice parts of town, and on one occasion, a man tried to snatch my handbag from my hands. Luckily, though frightened and shocked, I managed to hold on.

About 90 percent of my fellow commerce classmates at Wits were White, and it seemed to me that just about all of them had cars – some of the wealthier ones had quite nice cars, at that. Just about every one of them knew how to drive and had a driver's license, even if she or he didn't own a car.

As I approached my fourth year of university, I realized that I couldn't keep relying on public transportation because when I did my articles at an accounting firm, I would have to travel from one client to another. I had to learn how to drive, so I used some of my scholarship money awarded for tuition and accommodation to pay for driving lessons. This meant that I couldn't afford to live on campus anymore and had to move in with my parents back in Westbury. While they were happy to have me, I now had a lengthy, inconvenient commute to and from university every day, which cut down on my study time.

Unfortunately, driving did not come naturally to me, although I managed to get through the course at a private driving school and pass the licensing test. I then used the rest of my scholarship money as a down payment on a car, which I purchased just before I began working. Still I was not a very confident driver, not by a long shot, especially when driving in Johannesburg with its notoriously heavy traffic and aggressive drivers.

I hadn't been at work long when I had to drive – a lot – because my manager assigned me to my first audit. This was exciting, but the company I was auditing was quite a distance away, and getting there required driving on three or four different highways, which meant I'd have to be in the proper lane at the proper time to get on the interchanges. And I would have to do it daily for several weeks in a row.

It was a disaster! Looking back, it's kind of funny. Here's this twenty-two-year-old woman hunched over the steering wheel in her second-hand Ford Laser. She appears to possess the razor-sharp reflexes and daring of youth, but she feels like a lump of lead with her "driving brain" moving even slower than her weighted arms. She's nervously putt-putting slowly along the highway with cars whizzing by on both sides. Even the trucks are passing her, some of them zooming up right behind her before switching to a different lane and leaving her in the dust. Little trucks and giant rigs are all zooming by the frightened woman.

She sees the first interchange up ahead and flips on the turn signal, so she can change into the appropriate lane. But there's a truck right next to her, and it isn't going anywhere. Any other driver would probably speed up, pass the truck, and change lanes, but she's too scared to go "fast." Although she tries slowing down to let the truck pass, even the cars in the slow lane whiz by too fast for her to gently ease her way in, so she misses the interchange and winds up on the wrong freeway. This is before the days of GPS, so she drives down the wrong highway a bit before managing to get off, pull over, pull out her map book, figure out a new route, and get back on the highway. Slowly working her way back down the highway, cars and trucks flying by on both sides, she comes up to the next interchange and, once again, is too frightened to either speed up or slow down to get around the truck that's preventing her from making the necessary lane change. She misses the interchange once again!

This happened to me three times that first morning, and while humorous in retrospect, driving is still an issue today, two decades post-apartheid. Formerly oppressed people are still less likely to own cars[9] or have regular access to sharing-economy transport and

---

9 According to a survey by Statistics South Africa covering 30,000 households from April 2016 to March 2017, 19.8 % of Black households, 41.8 % of Coloured households, and 81.3 % of Indian households own a motor vehicle in working condition, compared to 94.2 % of White households. Source: "Vehicle ownership by gender, population – Stats SA." September 29, 2017. Accessible at http://www.wheels24.co.za/News/Guides_and_Lists/few-african-households-own-a-vehicle-in-working-condition-stats-sa-20170929. Viewed February 6, 2018.

more likely to depend on public transportation, which is notoriously inefficient and undeveloped in South Africa. This often means lengthy commutes with unreliable "delivery times," so we are more likely than our White colleagues to be late for work, which can be interpreted as not caring about work, and are therefore less likely to move ahead. In many cases, you can work around this issue, perhaps by leaving an hour earlier, but it's another problem the "others" have to deal with that Whites are usually not even aware of.

Most Whites are probably not aware of the fact that many "others" graduated from high school, reached university, or began working with quite a few "gaps" to fill. For some, the gaps were serious impediments to advancement, and they were forced to expend a great deal of extra time, effort, and often money to catch up. Even after leaving university, I continued to expand my horizons, and in my late twenties, I finally learned how to swim and ride a bicycle. Swimming and riding a bike may seem like trivial things – and certainly not necessary to be an accountant – yet to me, being able to swim a lap and ride a bike down the street were huge triumphs: it was as if I were making myself whole at last.

Many of my choices as an adult had to do with making up for what I lacked as a child. I chose to persist in filling these gaps and finally realized that there was one more choice to make: I had to stop treating myself as some project in need of more of this or more of that. It was time to accept my past just as it was, and to accept myself just as I am.

A Few Words on Grampa's "Other Wall"

Grampa was much more than the elderly man who built the wall to protect our Westbury house. He was friendly, talkative, and helpful. He read books on body building and worked out, so he was physically lean and athletic looking – but he was also sentimental, tearing up while watching sad movies or sharing something emotional. He visited our house on the weekends, drinking piping hot tea, and watching sports or *Noot vir Noot* – an Afrikaans television show on which participants had to guess the names of songs being played – with my parents. He also liked to have us over to his house to visit.

There's a picture of my grampa with my twin sister and me taken when we girls were about three years old. We're dressed in matching outfits – our Sunday best, complete with yellow check dresses, fancy hairpins, and long socks. We're standing right up against Grampa, one of us nestled against his right leg, the other against his left leg. He is very tall and towers over us. His hands rest lightly on our shoulders, holding us close.

It's a nice photo of a loving grandfather with "his little girls," a memento I'll cherish forever. It's also an essay on the insanity of apartheid, for Grampa looks like he came straight out of northern Europe. A person who knew nothing of the people in the photograph could be forgiven for wondering what this White, green-eyed, blond man was doing with two little Coloured girls. In fact, Grampa was half-White and half-Coloured, for his father was Welsh, while his mother was Coloured.

Since Grampa was born before the dawn of apartheid, before the racial classification and segregation rules had been hardened, he was able to "play White," to be registered as White, work as a White man with a White man's salary, go to a White hospital when he was ill, and otherwise lessen the pain of being one of the "lessers." But while Grampa could pass as White, Granny could not, for she was clearly Coloured. So they lived in a Coloured suburb of Johannesburg called Coronationville, an average Coloured suburb that was not the nicest but certainly much better than neighboring Westbury where we lived. Even though Grampa passed as White and earned a White salary, he wasn't particularly well off, for he worked in the building trade and went from one contract to another, often with a month or two of unemployment between contracts. Since Granny had lost her eyesight at the age of forty-three and was unable to work, she could not bring in a second salary, which they really needed to support their eight children. Grampa and Granny raised their eight children in a modest two-bedroom house. Some of their children looked White, and some did not. My mother did not. When Grampa developed bleeding hemorrhoids, he was able to go to a White hospital for surgery, which meant he received better care. But since he was in the White-only

Milpark Hospital, Granny could not visit him. Neither could my mother or several of her siblings. In fact, of Grampa's entire family, only one of his children, my Aunt Cynthia, was both White-looking and old enough to visit him in the hospital.

I knew nothing of this as a young girl and teenager. To me, Grampa was Grampa! One thing I remember is that he was convinced that my sister and I were smarter than any other children, and was so proud of a local press article stating that Julie-Ann Boggenpoel "is the top HoR matriculant in the Transvaal[10]. . . She finished sixth overall in the country. Her twin sister Jesmane . . . finished second in the Transvaal." Transvaal province had some four thousand Coloured, final-year high school students taking that exam. Grampa took it for granted that we would also be number one and two at university. I guess he didn't understand that it was quite another thing to be tops when competing with the best students from all over the country, the vast majority of whom were White and therefore had attended superior public and private schools. On several occasions after semesters at Wits wrapped up, Grampa asked, "Did you come first in the class?" and was surprised and a little disappointed to learn that I was "only" in the top group. Grampa truly believed that I was the best.

I said a little earlier that Grampa was able to lessen the pain of being a "lesser" by playing White, but it seems to me that you couldn't entirely escape this pain, for even if you successfully carried off the race-change charade, you always wondered if you would be caught. You couldn't casually chat with your White workmates or friends, for they might ask where you grew up or what school you went to, and answering truthfully might reveal your secret. You couldn't let them see any photographs of your family, for your dark-skinned parent, sibling, or cousin would give you away. And you couldn't be seen out and about with "one of your own," for Whites did not mix socially

---

10 HoR, which stands for House of Representatives, was an official South African body that, among other things, handled the education of Coloureds and the examinations for Coloured schools during apartheid. From 1910 through 1994, the Transvaal was a large province in the north-eastern portion of South Africa. After apartheid fell, Transvaal was divided into several smaller provinces.

with "others." How did you carry off the deception? Did you keep to yourself as much as possible to avoid questions? Or, instead, did you develop an elaborate cover story? Maybe you confided in a few trusted friends just to have someone to talk to? And how did it come to be that Grampa played White? Did he make that choice? Was it made for him, perhaps by his parents? Did it happen incrementally, as one event piled upon another?

I never asked Grampa about any of this; it never occurred to me to do so until now. And now I wonder, what were the walls limiting his life? He had leapt over the one that would have confined him to life as a Coloured man but then chose to climb back over it by marrying a Coloured woman. Could he have escaped entirely into the world of the White by marrying a White woman? His life would certainly have been much easier, for he could have lived with her in a White neighborhood, had White friends over for visits, and concocted a fictitious life story to hide the Coloured half of him. As it was, he had to hide much about himself. For example, he couldn't give his employer or a White hospital his address because they might realize he lived in a Coloured neighborhood. Instead, he used the address of a Coloured friend of his who was also playing White and living in a White neighborhood. And Grampa's choice of friends was limited to others like him, those who had one White and one Coloured parent; when he was with them, he didn't have to worry about being discovered. There was one thing that Grampa did that some others who were playing White didn't: if he was in the city and ran into a Coloured relative, he would openly greet them. This was dangerous, for if an employer or fellow-worker saw him doing so, he might be exposed and lose his job.

Grampa could have made a different choice, he could have left his past entirely behind. But that would have meant leaving behind his Coloured mother as well as those of his siblings, aunts, uncles, and cousins who were not light-skinned enough to play White. Which would have been worse: the pain of being Coloured or the pain of denying your mother? And what of the stress of living the lie? Suppose someone had seen through his deception, or suppose he and a White woman he might have married produced a Coloured child?

Grampa suffered the apartheid-produced pain of being the product of a mixed marriage. Did he also suffer the pangs of wondering what might have been had he chosen to keep going once he leapt over the wall, never looking back?

I wish I had asked. No, maybe not. Maybe it was better to let any thought of that, if he ever had it, lie still.

3

I FINALLY FORGAVE MY FATHER

MANY GREAT AND heroic stories of apartheid have been told: Nelson Mandela's twenty-seven-year imprisonment on Robben Island, where much of his time was spent at hard labor; the tragic death of Hector Pieterson, the twelve-year-old whose limp, bloodied body is seen being carried away by a fellow student during the Soweto student protests in a photograph printed in newspapers around the world; and many others.

Much less familiar are the ordinary stories of unknown men and women slowly ground down under the heel of apartheid, mundane tales of average people who wanted nothing more than to raise their children in nice homes and safe neighborhoods, to feel as though they were worthy and respected members of their communities, to share some good times with family and friends, and as the end approached, to look back and say it was all worthwhile.

But that was not to be, not for many who had the misfortune to be something other than White. I'm not speaking of the courageous firebrand activists or the writers who penned protest poems and songs, nor of the bomb-throwers who risked it all, or the emigrants who washed their hands of it all. Instead, I'm speaking of the regular folk who simply tried to get through the days and years, holding on to a few shreds of dignity and hoping that their children would somehow have better lives.

I said these were the stories, plural, of unknown women and men, but it would be equally correct to say it was a single story that played out in millions of variants. Each version was unique, yet as a whole, they were depressingly similar, for the key elements could be predicted: continually bombarded with messages – obvious and subtle, powerful and petty – that they were lesser, hobbled by a deliberately inferior education, kept from better jobs, deprived of adequate police protection, quite possibly belonging to a family broken apart by the search for work, and the list goes on. The all-too-common result was a life focused on little more than trying to get by.

This is one variant of the story, that of my father, Johnny Boggenpoel.

Daddy was born shortly before the dawn of apartheid in 1947, the second child of a woman who, while married to one man, conceived a child (Daddy) with another man who rapidly exited from her life, triggering a divorce from the first. All told, she produced eight children by five men, one of whom she married, and she later went on to marry a second husband. Although her relationship choices were extreme, they do point to an important issue in the Coloured community: broken families and out-of-wedlock babies. Although the community as a whole cherished marriage and stable families, the realities of being Coloured in South Africa at that time – including the lengthy periods of time that men might be away working, stretching into the months – encouraged broken families and unplanned, out-of-wedlock births. Moreover, since women were paid significantly less than men and had far fewer opportunities, there was a perverse incentive in some cases for women to seek security by having children with men to whom they were not married.

Daddy's mother, whom we called Mama, was a petite, attractive woman with deep blue eyes. She was multilingual, speaking excellent Xhosa, English, and Afrikaans. She spent long hours working in a Johannesburg garment factory and earned very little money, so when Daddy was less than a year old she delivered him into the care of her parents, who were living in Kliptown, a Coloured township in Soweto, south of Johannesburg. They had been forced to move there from a racially mixed suburb called Jeppe as the government began segregating the groups in preparation for the Group Areas Act, which made the segregation mandatory.

This law, officially passed by Parliament in 1950, was essentially an act of racial cleansing by which the Blacks, Coloureds, and Indians were forcibly removed from their homes and neighborhoods and shoved into other homes in different areas, sometimes close to where they had been living and sometimes far away. The impetus behind the act was to reserve the best land and best neighborhoods for the Whites, and it was successful in this regard. There was a major side-effect to this policy, however, which was to push the Blacks, Coloureds, and Indians away from the city centers and major industrial areas, forcing many of them to endure lengthy commutes to and from work. Sometimes it was a matter of hours to get to work and sometimes it took days, forcing many men to leave their families for weeks or months at a time, live in faraway places, and even then to endure lengthy commutes to work each day.

The act also ensured that while they were commuting and working, they had a sense of being in a sort of foreign territory, a place where things were more prosperous, safer, cleaner, and in every way better than their own neighborhoods. Among some of the work commuters and migrants, this spurred anger and resentment, but in many, it bred acceptance, a feeling of "we are lesser" that took root and grew in them slowly and so subtly that they never noticed. Soon enough, however, they had subconsciously embraced the idea that they were designed and destined to be less, to be worthy of less, and to receive less as a matter of course.

Mama was fortunate to be employed in a factory and only commuted from her township into the city center. Despite her steady, full-time employment, however, Mama did not earn enough to support a family. So, as her children were born, she cared for them for no more than a few years before delivering them to her parents and sister, just as she had done with Daddy. The only child she was able to keep with her was the youngest.

Daddy's early years with his grandparents, from six months to seven years, were peaceful and loving. Yes, he lived in a Coloured township, and yes, there was great upheaval as the Group Areas Act and other parts of apartheid were put in place, but his grandparents took good care of him and sheltered him as best they could.

Then, tragedy struck: Great-grandfather suffered a severe stroke that left him physically disabled and with not much time to live. And so my great-grandparents, along with Daddy and several other family members, moved to the family farm near Seymour in the Eastern Cape, where my great-grandparents wished to spend their final days. This was a piece of a much larger farm originally owned by one of Great-grandmother's ancestors, a Dutchman named De Klerk, and divided over the generations. In 1954, it consisted of numerous smaller farms, each about the size of a medium-sized shopping mall, owned by various De Klerk descendants. My great-grandparents' plot was large enough for them to grow *mielies* (corn), tobacco, onions, beetroot, and a few other crops and to have three or four donkeys and lots of chickens. Unfortunately, they could not grow enough crops or produce enough eggs and chickens to support a family, especially one that by this time consisted of Great-grandfather and Great-grandmother, Daddy, his four siblings (with one more to arrive soon), Daddy's Aunt Susan and her baby son, plus Daddy's Uncle Jacob and his girlfriend. Fortunately, both Great-grandfather and Great-grandmother had small retirement pensions from the state and Aunt Susan owned a truck, which she used as a large taxicab, taking farm families to and from town, the farm children to and from school, and hiring it out for weddings and to local rugby teams traveling to games. Between the pensions, truck-money, and money sent by Mama, the family got by.

When he moved to the farm, Daddy was a happy and content child who would have liked to play with others but wound up being a bit of a loner, for there were no children his age nearby. He was very attached to his grandmother: he slept in her bed, while bed-ridden Grandfather slept on a mattress on the floor in a different room, and Grandmother kindly kept the lamp on at night, for Daddy was afraid of the dark.

Daddy enjoyed life on the farm, despite the fact that it had no running water or well, that they used outhouses rather than flush toilets, and paraffin lights instead of gas or electric lights, all of which was common on Coloured farms back in the 1950s. With Great-grandfather incapacitated, Daddy began taking on chores at the age of eight and was excited and pleased to do so. Arising at five in the morning seven days a week, he performed various tasks before heading off to school – and he did even more chores on the weekends. One of his favorite duties was hitching two donkeys to a cart, placing some empty containers on it, and leading the donkeys to the stream, where he would fill the containers with water and return to the house. He also cleaned the yard, chopped and stacked firewood, helped bake bread, tended to the chickens, collected their eggs, and slaughtered them for family consumption.

Although the farm was not productive enough to produce cash crops, they had enough to eat and supplemented their diet by buying vegetables they did not grow from neighboring farms. They also had adequate clothing and a little bit extra to purchase necessities. Nearby White farms were more prosperous, with running water, windmills, more livestock, and more of everything. Perhaps they were better off because, back then, Afrikaner White farmers were assisted by the Land Bank, which provided generous subsidies to Afrikaner farmers during times of drought or poor production. But Daddy never thought about this – it was simply the way things were. Instead, he enjoyed being out in nature and working with his hands; he liked the change of rhythm from seed time to harvest time, the fresh air, the braying of donkeys and peeping of chickens, and the long walks to visit neighbors, many of whom were near or distant relatives.

Unfortunately, soon after they returned to the farm, Great-grandfather passed away. This was a real blow to Daddy, who looked upon his grandfather as his father and even called him Pa. He also thought of his grandmother as his mother and called her Ma, for he only saw his biological mother, whom he called by her first name, Annie, once a year when she visited the farm for one to three weeks, bringing toys and clothing for the children.

Life on the farm continued after Great-grandfather was buried, and three adult brothers who had a farm nearby and were nephews of my great-grandmother helped out to keep the farm running. In truth, they had been helping all along, for remember, Great-grandfather was physically disabled. The years passed quietly, and Daddy grew to be physically strong, quiet, and thoughtful. He enjoyed playing rugby with school friends and was quite good at it.

Then, when Daddy was thirteen years old, his grandmother

suffered a serious stroke and lingered for three months before she died. Thus ended what was perhaps the most idyllic portion of Daddy's life, a time when he was loved and cared for, was proud of the fact that he worked and contributed to the family, enjoyed the simple farm lifestyle, and flourished in school. Apartheid was not a serious issue to him, a young boy who was happy with his lot and never concerned himself with why certain others had it so much better. His fondest and happiest memories are from the farm.

With his grandmother's death, that phase of his life was over. Mama came from Johannesburg with her youngest to fetch him and his siblings, and they all took up temporary residence with Mama's cousin in Port Elizabeth, a large city in the Eastern Cape. Three months later, Mama rented a "cottage" for the family in Port Elizabeth. This was not the thatch-roofed, pastoral, and pleasant peasant-home you've read about in fairy tales. Instead, a cottage was essentially a little building consisting of one large room behind someone's house, with toilet facilities located in the main house. Cottages were very common in the townships due to the shortage of housing, and they were often cramped, tired-looking, and without a stove or ablution facilities. In this particular cottage, as in so many others, bathing facilities consisted of a large plastic bucket set behind a little curtain into which you poured buckets of water. Six months later, Mama moved the family to a proper, though small house, which had two bedrooms, a kitchen, a lounge, and an indoor bathroom.

Daddy adapted quickly to his new life, once again flourishing in school and impressing his teacher – he was proudly in the top five of the thirty students in his seventh grade class, and his favorite topics were math and history. He hoped to remain in school but money was very tight, so Mama took him out of school when he was fourteen and, through a neighbor, found a job for him in a shoe factory. Although extremely disappointed that his studies ended, he did his job diligently, sitting at a bicycle-like station for eight hours a day and pedaling a machine that stamped shoe sizes onto the soles. Eight hours seems like a long time to pedal, but he was young and energetic, and all that rugby playing must have strengthened his legs. Daddy's workmates were much older than he – in their twenties and thirties – so he grew up quickly.

For three years, he took the thirty-minute bus commute to work before pedaling for eight hours every day for a beginning wage that was just enough to buy a loaf of bread and some chips (French fries). When he was fifteen, he began buying cigarettes as well, developing a five-a-day habit that grew to twenty per day and continued for the next forty-two years. He commuted and pedaled for three years, with his salary slowly rising to the point where it was a small second income for a not-so-well-off Coloured family. Between what he and his mother earned – by this time, she worked out of the home as a self-employed dressmaker, securing customers on an irregular basis – the family got by.

Eager to earn more, he left the shoe factory and went to work in a General Motors car factory, where he fixed cars that had been improperly assembled on the line. An inspector would note what was wrong with the car, then Daddy would adjust or replace the bad parts. This was more interesting than pedaling a size-stamping machine all day. Unfortunately, after just six months, he was "retrenched," which is how we say laid-off in South Africa. Thankfully, another neighbor told him about an opening at Shatter Proof Glass, which made car windscreens and shopfront windows. So for the next four years, he worked at a big machine making "glass sandwiches." That is, he would lay out a piece of glass, place a sheet of shatter-proofing material on it, and put a second piece of glass on top. Then, he would stand the "sandwich" up on its end and feed it through a machine that fused everything together to create a single piece of shatter-proof glass. He did this for four years, eight hours a day, and gave all his wages to Mama, who gave him pocket money. Later, he went to work at a Ford plant, where he received parts, inspected them, set aside the defective ones, and took the rest to the body parts department.

By this time, he was being paid enough to buy the weekly groceries for a family of seven or eight. Yet, he was beginning to push against the upper limits, against the "concrete ceiling" every Coloured factory worker smacked into sooner or later. You see, there was only so far one could go – perhaps become a supervisor but nothing more – no matter how skilled and dedicated one might be. Coloureds were workers,

Whites were managers, and that was that. All of Daddy's bosses in the various places he had worked to this point were White. They treated him well in the sense that they never yelled at or physically abused him; indeed, some were quite pleasant and complimented him on his work. But the fact remained that he stood to one side of the line, they stood on the other, and he could never step over that line. This never troubled him, for to him, it was just the way things were.

Hoping to earn more one day, Daddy left Ford to become a carpenter's apprentice. This was a costly thing to do, for his pay immediately dropped to a small fraction of what it had been. But he was happy to be on a new track and spent the next year doing menial construction tasks and hauling and fetching things while learning the craft. After a year, he was promoted to assistant journeyman and two years after that to full-fledged journeyman construction carpenter. From there, he shifted to a roofing specialist firm called Bellsasbestos for which he installed ceilings and fixed roofs. He enjoyed this job, helping to build a school, post office, and housing development, and his manager, who was White, was friendly and gave Daddy extra responsibilities. He was now earning enough to support his own family. And so, close to age twenty-five, he moved out of his mother's house, married my mother, Patricia, and set up their own home in Korsten, a Coloured township in Port Elizabeth. Their home was actually an apartment building called "Tyre's Flat," which was perched above shops and stores. The neighborhood was fairly "nice", meaning it was not dirty or filled with gangsters. And since housing was scarce in the Coloured communities, my parents were forced to share this apartment with another couple. Luckily, it was a rather large apartment. Soon after, my parents moved to Salsoneville, Port Elizabeth, where my twin sister and I were born.

For the next few years, Daddy worked as a construction carpenter for a series of companies, always on a contract basis. This was common: you would be hired to work on a certain project and when that was finished, so were you. In the Eastern Cape Province, where separation between Whites and Coloureds was less strictly enforced, he often worked alongside Whites. Daddy had no problem with the Whites and they had none with him, although he did notice that the Whites always earned more than the Coloureds. It may be the same job, same number of hours, and same effort, but there was always a salary difference. Daddy accepted this as simply the way things were.

A big change came in 1975, when Daddy took on a contract to work at a uranium mine being constructed in Namibia, a bordering country to the north-west of South Africa. The mine was far away – about a two-day train ride from Port Elizabeth – and the conditions bleak in the scorching hot Namib Desert where the mine was located, but the large paycheck was enticing. By this time, my twin sister and I were two years old, so the extra money was welcome. For three months, he worked ten hours a day, seven days a week, with just one day off per month – and it wasn't exactly a festive day off, since he was living in the dormitories of a huge mine complex. Fortunately, Daddy wasn't working underground digging tunnels. Instead, he was above ground, employed by a major South African construction company called Murray & Roberts. Murray & Roberts was one of two companies that had been hired by the mine owners to handle the construction work necessary to create a major mining operation.

Daddy's job was to oversee the creation of concrete beams and columns. He began by cutting and arranging the wood used to create forms. He then supervised the men who poured concrete into the forms and smoothed it with a machine called a vibrator (essentially, a very large, electric egg-beater). The concrete was then left to sit and once it was dry, Daddy and the team stripped away the wood and stacked the newly created beams and pillars, which were soon taken away and used for various purposes. This, he has told me, was the hardest job he ever had – physically hard because it was unbearably hot and emotionally hard because there was rarely a break, and he was so far from home. The blunt truth is that Murray & Roberts exploited Daddy and the other Coloured workers, knowing that the firm was sheltered by apartheid. These workers had a simple choice: do what the boss told you to do, or leave. And so Daddy worked to the point of physical, emotional, and mental exhaustion. Many other workers left before their contracts ran out, but Daddy remained, determined to earn as much money as possible for his family.

After three months his contract was up, and he boarded the train back to South Africa, taking his single suitcase and a bag of tools. Instead of going to Port Elizabeth, where we were living, Daddy headed for Johannesburg, wanting to explore more financially lucrative work opportunities. Settling into his seat in the Coloured compartment of the train, he suddenly felt exhausted. You might think he would relax on the trip, but he couldn't. He couldn't settle down, and he couldn't sleep for more than a few minutes at a time. He could, however, hear voices. People he knew were not there were talking. Not to him, not telling him to do certain things or threatening him; just talking. A constant chatter carried on by people who weren't there. After a while he was literally alone in the compartment, for all the other passengers had exited, but those voices continued murmuring away. The longer it went on the more he worried, for there had never been the slightest hint of any mental problem until that very moment. Finally, he dozed off. When he awoke, he thought things might now be all right until he noticed that someone had broken the lock on his suitcase and stolen much of his clothing and some of his work tools from his bag. They had taken his wallet and train ticket, as well. Then, the conductor came by to punch his ticket and, upon learning that Daddy didn't have one, threatened to put him off the train at the next stop. Daddy was devastated by the thought of being dumped off the train. Luckily, the crooks hadn't taken his camera or sandals, so he was able to sell these items at a huge discount to a fellow passenger, earning enough money to buy a ticket, which he gave to the conductor.

Finally arriving in Johannesburg, he went to the hospital – the Coloured hospital, which was not as well-equipped or staffed as White hospitals. In the United States, the recently deceased Jim Crow laws holding down Blacks had at least made a pretense of being "separate but equal." In South Africa, there was no such charade. At the hospital, the doctor diagnosed Daddy as having suffered a nervous breakdown, gave him some medication that left him feeling fatigued and foggy-brained, and told him to stop drinking. That was easy to do, for while away on the Murray & Roberts contract, he drank two glasses of wine a day, plus the occasional beer.

Six months later, feeling fine, he started drinking wine and beer again. This was on weekends at the home of a relative who ran a *shebeen*, which was a house where alcohol could be sold informally. Daddy drank one bottle of wine every Saturday and one every Sunday for six months at the *shebeen*, and then he began hearing voices again and imagining things. He returned to the Coloured hospital where he was again evaluated by a psychiatrist. The diagnosis was the same: a nervous breakdown. This time, though, there was an interesting twist. The doctor said the problem stemmed from the fact that Daddy never knew who his father was, and this had haunted him his entire life. Indeed, since the time he was a teenager, he had wondered who his father was, but Mama would never tell him. It got to the point where he would drink in hopes of ginning up the courage to ask her, but he never got up quite enough nerve to do so. He failed to do so until she died in 1988, and then it was too late.

Following this relapse, Daddy, feeling confused, tired, and knowing he needed help, was admitted to a Coloured mental institution in Johannesburg for a brief stay. He recovered quickly and returned to work, but soon began drinking again. He then suffered a more severe breakdown, imagining things like the house was burning down, and sometimes seeming to speak gibberish. This was in 1977, when I was four years old.

And now followed nine months of hospital stays and discharges, some with the consent of the doctors and some without. Most of the details are unimportant, for the story of his treatment had already been outlined by apartheid. To begin with, fewer Coloureds in distress would even bother seeking treatment because they had to continue trying to support their families. Any disability pension a Coloured person might be granted would be decidedly less than the one allotted to a White person with a similar work history, and since the Coloured had been making less all along, he almost certainly had less money in reserve to fall back on. If he went for treatment, he did so knowing there were fewer doctors and other personnel at the Coloured hospitals, older and less well-equipped facilities, less treatment in terms of time and therapy, and less in every other way.

Let me give you two quick examples. At one point, Daddy spent six months at a state-run facility in the town of Fort Beaufort in the Eastern Cape. All of the doctors there were White, while the nurses were Black, and the Black, Coloured, and White patients were kept separate. Daddy and the other Coloureds were given a bland, inexpensive diet of corn and beans, the occasional green vegetable, and slices of cooked pumpkin, complete with hard outer skin and seeds. Once a week, there was a special treat: a piece of meat. Daddy intensely hated the food.

One day, Daddy happened to go into the kitchen, where he saw meals being readied. On one set of preparation tables was the corn, beans, and other foods he recognized as his regular fare. On another set of tables sat nice plates of meat, mashed potatoes, and veggies. "Who got that food?" he wondered. A woman working in the kitchen told him, "That's for the White patients."

Not only were the Coloureds given lesser food, they were also forced to work on behalf of the Whites. Five days a week following breakfast, a supervisor rounded up the Coloured patients and took them off premises to houses belonging to the White hospital managers. There, they would pull weeds, plant things, and otherwise work for three hours for no pay. Was this part of their therapy? If so, why did they only do it at the houses of White managers? Why not on the hospital grounds in a protected environment? And if it was therapy, why didn't the White patients also pull weeds?

After just one month at Fort Beaufort, Daddy saw that a gate had been left open and quickly walked out, heading down the road to the nearby town. Twenty minutes later, he was in town hoping to find the train station and figure out how to get a ticket back to the farm where he spent those wonderful six years during his childhood. His thoughts were muddled by the powerful medication he was being given; he didn't seem to realize there was no way for him to buy a ticket, but he knew for sure that he wanted to go back to that place where he had felt loved and cared for, where apartheid had not hammered away at him day after day, and where his future was full of possibilities – or so it seemed to him back then. Unfortunately, his path to the train station had taken him right past the hospital manager's house, and the manager, who happened to be in his front yard, recognized the khaki hospital uniform and called for an ambulance, which arrived quickly, collected Daddy, and promptly took him back to the corn and beans, weed pulling, and heavy medication.

Finally after six months, which felt to him like a year, he returned home (which by this time was Johannesburg) and began working at a government-owned factory called Service Products in an industrial area of Johannesburg known as Crown Mines. This was in 1979, when he was thirty-two years old. His doctors had admonished him not to return to work as a construction carpenter because the heavy medication he was on would make working on ladders and roofs dangerous. But he needed to earn money. Fortunately, a relative suggested he work at Service Products, which was designed specifically for disabled Coloured workers and soldiers. And so he did, working dutifully for Service Products over the next seventeen years in – at various times – the kitchen, woodshop, textile shop, and even the medical department, where he helped the doctor dispense medications. Depending on where he worked, he would rise at five or six in the morning, get ready, walk to the train station, take the train, and finally walk to the plant, a one-hour commute each way. All of the managers were White, and his paycheck was small. He was despondent about working for so little money – just enough to cover the weekly groceries for the family – and over knowing he could never be a construction carpenter again. But he soldiered on.

In 1995, at the age of forty-eight, he was given an early retirement for medical reasons and has since received a very small monthly government pension check. His state disability grant comes to half of what he was earning at Service Products, so he can now buy half of the family's weekly groceries. He should also have had a regular pension from Service Products and a comfortable one at that, for he worked for them for seventeen years. It was and remains standard for South African companies to deduct a portion of an employee's paycheck and put it in a pension fund along with a contribution from the company. But this was not done for the Coloured workers at Service Products – at least not then – so Daddy and all the other disabled Coloured people who worked there are forced to rely on meager government pensions. And Daddy has long suffered a partial hearing impairment in one ear caused by exposure to the loud machines at Service Products, yet another of the many insults and injuries he has had to endure.

For several years after retiring, Daddy did some ad-hoc carpentry work as opportunities came his way. His biggest job, however, was caring for Granny, my mother's mother, when she came to live with us. He assigned himself this chore in 2002, when we were living in a nice home in Discovery, Roodepoort, the one I had purchased for my parents in 1999. Although still relatively junior in my career, I was able to buy my parents a nice house in a safe neighborhood, the kind of house they had wanted to raise their children in.

Unable to afford both the house and my own apartment, I stayed with them and, in 2002, shortly after my grandfather passed away, I insisted that Granny come live with us. With her husband of fifty-eight years gone and her eyesight lost decades before, it made sense. The house wasn't large enough to give Granny a separate room, so I invited my precious granny to move into my room, where we literally shared a bed.

Daddy, who had long since given up drinking and smoking, made it his personal mission to take care of Granny. Her ankles were terribly swollen, so on the advice of the doctor, Daddy took her for a morning walk every day. The swelling went down, and they continued these daily walks. He also took her out to the patio in the afternoons and sat with her listening to the birds singing, prepared all her meals, and otherwise treated her as if she were his own mother. In fact, Granny preferred to call upon Daddy to assist her, even if my mother (her daughter) happened to be home.

He faithfully did all this for five years until Granny passed away.

Anger, Gratitude

Daddy is now seventy-one years old and though partly bald and partly grey-haired, he looks and feels good. The difficult years of distress and heavy medication are long past, so he is energetic and alert. He walks briskly to the shops and to the bus stop for his commutes to the shopping mall. He attends church regularly, is friendly with the neighbors, and helps them out. That help once went beyond a little carpentry to assisting an ailing White neighbor with errands and other care before he passed away. Also, Daddy is a huge help with my errands and tasks.

To this day, Daddy harbors no anger over apartheid and neither does my mother, for both feel that this was simply the way things were, and you did your best to get along. That's certainly a positive attitude, and mixed in with the positivity is a large dose of acceptance. But that's what apartheid was designed to produce: a huge pool of accepting, submissive, subservient "others" who genuinely believed they were lesser, deserving of less, and willing to accept less of everything so that the Whites might be superior and better off. In a sense, apartheid was a massive welfare system for Whites, keeping 90 percent of the population out of the best jobs and off the best land, all but cut off from good education, courts and legislature, and working all the lesser jobs so that the Whites, including those who were not really qualified, might have the better jobs and lives.

I wasn't angry about apartheid when I was young. Instead, I was angry at Daddy because I felt that he didn't provide for us properly and that we were terribly poor as a result. I was angry because we lived in a gang- and drug-infested neighborhood where people made fun of my battered school case and my often-ill-fitting school uniform. I was angry because Daddy could not control his alcohol consumption. I was angry because Daddy couldn't be the energetic father who would take me for long walks; the wise father who would delight me with his knowledge; or the strong father who would wrap his arms around me and make me feel safe. He couldn't teach me how to ride a bicycle, swim, or drive a car. We didn't even have a bicycle or a car, and I blamed that on him, too. I blamed him for all this and much more.

I never said any of this to Daddy, but I'm sure he felt it, if not always, at times. I know he felt the anger my mother occasionally directed at him, for she, who had not completed high school, was forced to be the main earner for a family of five in an era where women were paid significantly less than men – and Coloured women less than White women. After a long day at work topped off by long train commutes to and from, she sometimes took out her frustration on him.

And so Daddy was a double victim. First, he was abused by the system that doomed him to a "lesser life" as a Coloured person, that allowed Murray & Roberts to work him past his limit and push him to a breakdown, and that did not provide him with the best care or a living wage while he was working at Service Products. What he received was less than White men who worked at identical jobs at similar factories designed for disabled White workers. Second, Daddy was forced to absorb the misdirected resentment and anger that sometimes spilled out of his wife and children. They – we – were angry because of the system, but that system was some ethereal thing out there, somewhere. We couldn't be angry at it, so we were angry at him.

Daddy, too, was angry. He was angry at himself for having made what he felt were poor choices, for being unable to support his family himself, and for being unable to fulfill the promise he made to Mummy when they married – that he would earn enough money to allow her to return to school and earn a high school diploma. He was sorry that he was unable to make the future as bright as it had seemed to them back then when they married.

My Sorrow

Writing this book has required me to ask my father a lot of questions about things that were never discussed in the family. I knew he worked on the farm as a boy and left school early to take a job, but I never realized he was forced to take on major responsibilities for supporting his siblings when he was so young. I never knew about the exhausting and punitive working conditions at Murray & Roberts that triggered the first breakdown, how much the medications robbed him of energy and clarity, and how frightening it was to hear voices in your head. I never knew he was such a proud man, only admitting to me now that he was forced to retire from Service Products because of his illness – back then, he told us that he had chosen early retirement.

And I never realized that I had misdirected my anger. Fortunately, Daddy didn't absorb my anger and only talks about how proud he is that his children have done so well. He has confessed that he felt bad about not being able to provide for us, and I wonder how much pain he is hiding, to this day. How could it not have hurt to know that your daughter was struggling with school bullies, with growing up, with finding her footing in what was then the White world of business, and be unable to help? How could it not have hurt to know that while she was growing up dealing with the pleasures and pains of life, both ordinary and extraordinary, he stood on the sidelines, too fatigued by medication to help?

How could this not have hurt such a loving man? And now that I know all that he endured, how can I not see him in a new light? He quietly bore the "slings and arrows of outrageous fortune," never questioning, never complaining, rising every morning and placing one foot in front of the other as he moved along the narrow and rutted path life had set out for him. Whatever the job, whatever the conditions, whatever the low pay given simply because of his skin color, he sought to provide for his family. Even when all he could do was pay for the weekly groceries, when it would have been easy to give up, he continued, placing one foot in front of the other, every day, without fail. How can I not love and admire him?

Journey's End

The happiest part of Daddy's life was those six years he spent on the farm. Cared for by loving grandparents he called Ma and Pa, surrounded by family on adjacent farms, flourishing in school, proud of the many chores he performed daily, working with his hands and living in rhythm with nature, he felt at peace.

When his grandmother died, he was yanked out of this idyllic life and began a long journey through time; through various workplaces, homes, and hospitals; and through apartheid. He survived, though he bears many scars of the journey, some undoubtedly still afflicting him in ways no one recognizes, for he, like so many others, only survived by pushing pain down so deep it could no longer be seen and did not have to be dealt with. So they thought.

As I was writing this chapter, I remembered that soon after I purchased the home where my parents now live, Daddy mentioned a few times that he wanted us to name the house. I didn't pay much attention to the idea at the time, thinking it odd to name a house. It's not a majestic mansion like Cardiff Castle – it's just a house.

I reminded Daddy of this and asked him what name he had in

mind for the house. "Journey's End," he replied.

It makes perfect sense, for living in this house is the end of a journey for Daddy. Apartheid is long gone, and he can now hold his head up high, knowing that he is the equal of any man. The last relapse into breakdown happened many years ago, and he hasn't had a drink or smoked a cigarette in too many years to remember. His three children got the education he was denied; indeed, they are all university educated. They have all had the opportunity to travel and live abroad, and the two older ones are well into satisfying, professional careers. He spent many years taking care of Granny, just as his grandparents had once cared for him, and he and Mummy are now comfortable and content. He feels as if he is a worthy and respected member of the community. He shares good times with family and friends. One day, as he faces the end of his journey on this earth, I hope he will look back and say it was all worthwhile.

Daddy recently said that he loves the home and wants to stay there. I hope he remains there for a long time, savoring his success.

4

LINGERING EMOTIONS

WHEN I FIRST thought of going to the Amazon jungle, I imagined exploring the lush tropical forest under a canopy of impossibly green trees, watching the brilliantly colored macaws gather by the hundreds to peck and eat clay off sheer cliff walls, and participating in various self-discovery workshops. This was October 2015, and I was going on an "Amazon Resilience Journey" to Peru. Our international group had a nice mix of workshops and outdoor activities planned for the nine-day stay. At our very first workshop, the leader, Stanford Professor Julia Novy-Hildesley, began by asking us to describe a challenging experience we each had to overcome.

I was the second one to speak and began relating what I thought would be a five- or six-minute version of my life story. I don't know if I was even three sentences into it before I began crying – really sobbing, tears flowing uncontrollably down my cheeks. I tried to tell these people whom I barely knew about that battered school case I had carried for so many years and how classmates laughed and said that it looked like it had been through both World War I and II. I wanted to tell them about apartheid and my father's illness and Westbury and so much more, but I couldn't choke out another word.

I just sat there sobbing, feeling as if I was crying for everything that happened to me. And even though I was surrounded by near-strangers, it felt so right to cry in front of them. I could cry because I didn't have to be perfect for them. All the suppressed pain I had been unable to express while growing up, going to school, and working my way up the ladder – all the pain generated by the pressure of having to break the cycles of poverty that had imprisoned my family for so long – suddenly came roaring out, along with all the shame I felt for being a poor and downtrodden girl under the thumb of apartheid. It was pain that I still felt to that day, despite the fact that by every objective measure, I had triumphed. We were *all* triumphant survivors of our past. So why wasn't I celebrating instead of sobbing?

I had not realized there was so much pain stuffed down inside of me. And I never would have guessed that I had to leave South Africa before I could release it.

Many of us are very good at suppressing our emotions. I suppose it's a defense mechanism that protects us from either exploding in rage or curling up into a ball and withdrawing from life. Suppression may have been especially important during apartheid, for we had to be strong to survive, and there was never time to reflect or indulge in commiseration. Unfortunately, those lingering emotions often fester, growing more toxic over time. And they can explode at unexpected times.

Certainly, I'm not the only one who experienced this. Others did, including my sister. We marched through apartheid in lockstep. We were even together in the public library at the age of nine, reading our favorite books with a bunch of other innocent little kids, when tear gas canisters came flying through the window and exploded on the floor, filling the room with noxious fumes. Students from our local high school were protesting against apartheid. Police were chasing – and undoubtedly beating – high schoolers who dared to demand an end to apartheid. Hearing screams, I glanced outside the library door at a mass of high school protesters frantically running away from the police and past the library before the gas canisters came flying in.

Our paths began to diverge when we began university, as she studied to become a medical doctor while I focused on becoming a chartered accountant. Like me, she was one of the few Coloureds in her program and wound up making friends with Jews, Greeks, Afrikaners, and more. My sister moved to Australia in 2002, where she has worked extensively with the urban aboriginal community, which has some issues in common with South African Coloureds, including alcoholism, teenage pregnancy, feelings of marginalization, and dispossession of the land. There are also some cultural similarities, such as respect for elders and similarity of body gestures in communication. Like me, she had not really dealt with any lingering emotions, for she was focused on getting an education, becoming a professional, and finding her place in life with her family. And like me, she was participating in a workshop when the negative emotions she had not processed came pouring out. This was in November 2014, about a year prior to my own experience.

I felt really traumatized. I had no idea that living in South Africa had affected me so. The question that triggered me was where we are from, and what had happened to the original owners of the land. I had not considered this growing up because life was so difficult that we took each day as it came. Then came university, and medical school, and work, and family. I never had time to look back, emotionally, and wonder about where I came from. I was so busy dealing with the here and now.

I had a brief and scary mental image of being physically present and witnessing a dispossession as White authority figures entered my great-grandmother's home in Albertville. This was a mixed-race suburb where she lived and owned a home, and that was declared White-only in the 1950s. She was gravely concerned about the impending forced removal. She actually died before it happened, but the rest of the family was forcibly removed from their home and community. I didn't experience this, for I hadn't been born yet, and great-grandmother wasn't actually forced out because she was dead. Yet somehow, this image of her being dispossessed of her home became the focus of all my pain, and this pain focused me on my identity.

I lost my appetite for a week; I was depressed and obsessed about these questions. It didn't make sense to me; I couldn't understand why I felt that way. I saw a psychologist for a few sessions, who told me that I was going through grief and loss not just for that incident, but for all the wounds in my life. The counseling was successful, starting a journey of healing and wholeness which is now complete. This was supplemented by support from my family and work colleagues, Christian

> *faith, and help from friends including an aboriginal friend. In the course of this introspection, I became more aware of and nostalgic for my tribal ancestors: the Khoisan people, the original inhabitants of the land. Somehow in that moment, I felt my own trauma and, vicariously, the trauma of the aboriginals as well.*
>
> *I never knew all that pain was there. Why did it take twelve years after leaving South Africa for it to hit me? I can't explain.*

Frozen by Regret

My sister and I shoved our emotions as far down as we possibly could, though it could never possibly be deep enough. We may not have been consciously aware of these emotions, but they were always there, simmering away, influencing our thoughts and actions until they finally boiled over. Other people are aware of their negative emotions; they feel them and don't like them. They know these lingering emotions are influencing them, maybe powerfully so, but neither suppress nor resolve them. Perhaps they cannot; perhaps they will not.

Sometimes, negative emotions are both suppressed and seeping, by which I mean that the person's suffering seems to be unrelated to the suppressed emotions until something makes it clear that they are connected.

My second-cousin Anneline Bradford (née Mordaunt) was raised in a Coloured township south of Johannesburg called Eldorado Park. It was run down and infested with gangs. Annie had almost no exposure to Whites in her early years, for it was rare to see a White person in the township – she only met one White woman, a friend of her mother's, who visited once a month. But she was well aware of the Whites, for when her parents took the family to Johannesburg to visit the library or go shopping, they would see benches with signs that said only Whites could sit there. They saw similar signs on the stores and at the beaches.

> *I didn't understand apartheid at that age, but I knew that the Whites had the best beaches, restaurants, and so on. I thought*

Whites were somehow special, because they had the best. That belief began to change as I grew older and learned more about the world. My father would come home from his job as a car parts salesman for General Motors and talk about how hard he worked. His boss, who could barely read and write, was White. Dad had finished school, knew more, and could do the boss's job better but could never be promoted to manager. And my mother, who worked in a bank, would sometimes train new White employees who would, in a few months' time, be her boss – but she could never be promoted.

At first I thought that White people must be better because they had better jobs. But later on, that didn't sound right: If Whites were less educated, why did they get the better jobs?

Annie graduated from university, became a psychologist, and moved to New Zealand in 2009. A fair number of South Africans, many of them White, have moved to New Zealand and Australia, so it's not unusual for a South African seeking psychological counseling to ask to see a South African psychologist. And many of the Whites who do so are surprised to see a Coloured woman when they come in for their first session.

When some of them see me, they instantly say, "We were never racist in South Africa." Clearly, they carry a lot of guilt over what happened. I reply, "Not all White people were racist under apartheid," and that usually resolves the issue. But there was one woman who carried a tremendous amount of guilt and shame concerning her ancestors and the way they oppressed the others. She didn't realize this; she didn't connect it to her depression and other symptoms.

She was very tearful, extremely sorrowful. She said to me, "My forefathers have caused a lot of harm." She spoke of her longing to return to South Africa, missing nature, and the authenticity of the African people, but felt she had no future there. And she was terribly burdened by a sense that because she was White, she had been part of the oppressive regime.

In one of our sessions, she apologized to me for what Whites had done under apartheid. I replied, "On behalf of all

> *Black people, I accept your apology. I forgive you and your ancestors."*
>
> *I wasn't sure why I said this, or how she would respond, but she seemed almost instantly relieved. When I saw her the next week, she was much less depressed, and her guilt and shame had given way to a more light-hearted manner. At a follow-up session a month later, she told me that her depression had vanished, and she was better able to think of New Zealand as her home.*

I wonder how many cases of depression, anxiety, social fears, and other problems are not what they seem to be? How many are manifestations of race-related issues and emotions that have never been resolved? And how long might it take to do so?

Moving Forward in Hope

The stories above illustrate what may happen when you have not dealt with negative emotions, which is why I believe that all negative emotions should be addressed and resolved, and if possible, used to spur one on to make positive change. In addition to my personal life, I've also needed to grapple with lingering emotions in the workplace. I found that others went through similar experiences, and that positive change is best achieved with others.

Two decades ago, when I was a young article clerk eager to gain experience and earn the hours necessary to qualify as a chartered accountant, I used to keep an eye on the big board hanging in one of the corridors at the international auditing firm where I was clerking. The names of all the article clerks from my department were written on this board, one under the other, and to the right of the names was a series of columns, one for each month. These columns served as a sort of work calendar. If a clerk was given an assignment for the month of January, the January slot next to his name would be filled in with the name of the assignment. With just a quick glance you could tell, for example, that Peter was slated to do the X company audit in January, followed by the Y company and Z company audits, and then others, meaning he was going to be busy until the end of the year. The more months that were filled in, the busier an article clerk would be.

Most of the months next to the names of the White article clerks were filled in – but not those next to the names of the Coloured and Black clerks. Every so often, I would look at all the blank months next to my name, then trudge through the company offices knocking on managers' doors, smiling, and brightly saying, "I have spare time on my calendar. Do you have any assignments I can work on for you?"

The answer was almost always the same: "We'll see what comes up and get back to you." I would smile again as I made my exit, knowing that the odds of anyone getting back to me were not in my favor.

Those excursions through the office always left me terribly weary. I felt like a beggar, going door to door pleading for work when my White counterparts had so many assignments they could hardly keep up. I did get work during my first year, but they were typically ad hoc, fill-in assignments that did not allow me to grow with the project. This was important, for in the first year of articles, you served as the trainee accountant on the audit team, in the second year as the senior trainee, and in your third year as the senior accountant, working closely with senior staff of the company you were auditing as well as with the audit partners in your own firm. If you didn't get assigned to various audits in your first year – on a permanent basis, not as a quick fill-in – there was less chance you would rise to become the senior trainee and senior accountant, work your way up the ladder, master the intricacies of auditing in a major firm, culminating when you led multiple large audits with a path toward becoming a senior manager and later partner at the audit firm. In truth, I was happy to have any assignment but worried that I would not have the growth trajectory that I needed for the full three years of articles. When we Coloured and Black clerks did get assignments, they tended to be for government entities such as a state-owned utility company. This was nice, but confining us to state-owned entity audits wouldn't give us the range of experience we would need to grow our business acumen.

There were not a lot of Coloured or Black chartered accountants in South Africa back then, just a few years after the fall of apartheid. We "others" were not encouraged to become one; on the contrary, we were actively discouraged. As a result, there were no Coloured or

Black chartered accountants serving as my superiors when I began my training, and relatively few Coloured and Black article clerks. I felt like a misfit during those early years in my profession, often being the only "other" in the room. It was a lonely, isolating experience. Yes, we Coloured and Black clerks shared a camaraderie and used to joke about the blank space next to our names. Yet there was no senior worker to whom I felt comfortable turning to for advice and support. And I felt that I had to be near perfect, lest I be judged inferior.

I later discovered that I wasn't the only one who felt so all alone. Sindi Koyana, who was named by the *Financial Mail* as one of South Africa's Twenty Most Powerful Businesswomen, told me, "Having qualified as a chartered accountant at a very early age, I battled to be allocated to certain audit clients who refused to be audited by a Black woman. I remember arriving at a client in the morning and within a few hours, I was called back to the office because the client threatened to cancel the engagement. Fortunately, Deloitte was already on a transformation plan and engaged the client on a principle basis, and I was put back to the client."

Neo Phakama Dongwana, the first Black African woman to become a partner at the KPMG Cape Town office and the daughter of slain apartheid activist Chris Hani, describes her experience: "I was introduced to the CEO of a client as the new audit partner. This client, a middle-aged Afrikaner man, could not hold back his dismay and exclaimed, 'A Black woman partner . . . now I've seen it all!'"

Gugu Sepamla, a Black woman whom *Forbes* pronounced one of the "Top 10 Most Powerful and Influential Women in Africa," faced a different kind of struggle. "I'm an anomaly, for my success in the corporate world was aided by White male mentors who supported me, pushed me, and remained interested in my growth. The flip side of this is the Black males and White women who have blocked me at every step. Prejudice from Black males has come in the form of reminding me to know 'my place.' From White females, it's come in the form of them throwing documents at my face in front of colleagues, speaking down at me, and dropping phones on me!"

Precious Sibiya, inaugural board member of the African Women Chartered Accountants Association, was working through her articles with a large international auditing firm when she was notified that she was being sent to North America for a JIT program; that is, she was being seconded for a few months to another of the firm's offices outside of South Africa. This may sound impressive until you learn that all the other article clerks were given three months' notice and allowed to pick the city and even the specific office where they would be sent to work and train. Precious was only given one month's notice and was not allowed to make the selection. All the others were Whites and Indians – she was the only Black.

Like many "others," these women and I suffered emotionally, and many of us carry our pain to this very day. For many of us, the sting of rejection, the fear of failure, and the memory of having to work harder than others just to be seen as "good enough" lingers. Today, one of the ways we address our pain is by easing the path for the next generation. We turn our hurt into hope by offering leadership development, scholarships, and mentoring to women of color who are studying to become chartered accountants or are in the early years of their careers.

We do this through a private corporation called the African Women Chartered Accountants Investment Holdings Company[11] (AIH) of which we are directors and in which we are investors. The money we've pooled has been invested in many businesses, and a portion of the profits is allocated to the African Women Chartered Accountants Association[12], a sister non-profit organization that handles scholarships, mentoring and other support.

AIH has another purpose: to accumulate wealth. That may sound selfish rather than altruistic, but it addresses one of the problems we all wrestled with when we were young, an issue that for many lingers as a psychic pain: poverty. Apartheid was structured to reserve as much wealth as possible for Whites. Blacks and Coloureds couldn't accumulate wealth from our wages, which were often just enough to

---

11 For more information, please refer to the website http://www.awcainvest.co.za/web/index.asp.

12 For more information, please refer to the website https://www.awca.co.za/.

keep a family going. The lack of extra cash in the Black and Coloured communities meant we weren't making money on the stock market, purchasing investment properties, or investing in business deals, and we weren't setting aside money every year to send our children to top-quality schools and universities. It was all about getting by.

For me, today, accumulating wealth is not about buying fancy cars and comforts. It's about the ability to make choices, an opportunity my parents never had. It's about not feeling so constrained, as I did when in poverty. It's about expanding my ability to learn and explore, to go to off-the-beaten-track countries, to see great art, to expand my horizons and life experiences. And it's about being able to empower and pass the gift of choice on to the next generation.

Even as we shareholders of AIH help others we help ourselves, for at our board meetings and other gatherings we can be entirely ourselves. During those precious hours, we don't feel that we are being scrutinized under a microscope, that we must be perfect lest "they" think less of "us." We're just sisters who walked the same difficult road and now look back on it with some tears, some laughter, and a burning desire to make that journey less difficult for others.

Sisterhood Soothes Emotions

There's one final thing that AIH is to me: a way to help people deal with their lingering emotions, whether they be suppressed, seeping, or even spewing out.

I believe that every time I get together with my sisters on the board, every time we laugh or cry, we release a little of our lingering emotions. Every time we review our investments and see they have risen, we feel as if we have increased our options as well as our opportunities to learn, explore, and grow. Every time we talk about helping another person or review the progress of those we've been helping, we create new, positive emotions in ourselves, which are, over time, shared with those we assist.

We can't change the past and may never completely deal with the emotions that linger. However, we can always and constantly build toward a new future, one in which everyone has hope and opportunity.

BRIDGING FOR AUTHENTIC CONNECTION

IN 2013, I was serving as a member of the board of a South African state-owned entity. One day, we met for a social dinner at a golf course in Pretoria. The twenty-five or so of us sat down together in a private room. Most of the board members were Black.[13] I only remember one White person, who was a man.

Speeches were made and formalities dispensed with. Before we began eating, the White man stood up, smiled gently, and said, "Being here, I couldn't help but think that twenty years ago, you would not have been permitted to play golf here – you would have been denied access to the whole country club, in fact. That was wrong. Today, as we gather in this room together, I feel sad about South Africa's history. It was wrong. I'm so glad we've made such progress."

I was heartened by this simple yet elegant example of bridging. In just a few sentences, he reached across the race line to connect with us all. What he said wasn't forced or required. He simply stood before us and stated, in so many words, "I care about you as human beings. I recognize the struggle you endured and the pain you felt. Knowing that you were hurt then, hurts me now."

What this man said stands in stark contrast to what others have said or suggested to me out of the blue on more than one occasion: "I

---

13 From this chapter onwards, I am using "Black" to collectively refer to all Africans, Coloureds, and Indians, in line with current legislation and practice in South Africa.

had nothing to do with apartheid."

That statement instantly throws up a wall between us, and I struggle to reply. That is, I know how to politely whisk the conversation off in a new direction, but I am not sure what motivates this defensive statement or how to respond to it. This typically happens when I am chatting socially with someone I know through business. We're not talking about apartheid or race relations, so why bring it up? Is he feeling bad about what happened in a general sense or because a relative was part of the apartheid regime? Is the statement genuine, or is he trying to curry favor with me?

What bothers me most about this statement is that it is a denial of my humanity. Even if the other person is sincere, he is not treating me as an individual. I am just one of those "others" who received the bad treatment he is washing his hands of. He says, "I had nothing to do with apartheid," but what I hear is this: "I don't want to hear anything about apartheid from you. I have no idea whether or how apartheid affected you, and my main focus is my own self-preservation."

I suppose he wants me to reply, "Yes, I know you're not responsible and hold absolutely nothing against you." Saying this would feel contrived and would not help us develop an authentic connection.

Sometimes, on the other hand, I'll meet someone, and she will say, "I know apartheid must have been hard for you" or something similar. Instantly, I feel a connection with her. I feel that she is seeing me as an individual and recognizing the struggle that I and all Blacks went through. She is reaching out to affirm and validate my experience.

The irony is that we all suffered because of apartheid. This was obviously so for Blacks, but the Whites did not emerge unscathed, either. They have been left to engage in an internal struggle of reconciling guilt from the atrocities of apartheid with their decision to be South Africans living in South Africa.

Here's another example. I'm sometimes asked by South African Whites what high school I attended and what other countries I've been to. I perceive this as an attempt to figure out whether I'm a "qualified Coloured" who knows what I'm doing, or an "affirmative-action Coloured." The assumption is that if I went to a private school I'm well educated, but if I went to a Coloured public school, I might not be. As for travel, the idea is that if I haven't traveled much outside South Africa, I'm probably less able. Remember, most "others" could not afford to travel out of the country during apartheid, so if you did, you probably had more money, went to a better school, and were more upper-class.

As it happens, I've lived on three continents and have traveled to nearly seventy different countries, which is "good," but I attended Coloured public elementary and high schools, which is "bad." So I guess that makes me a fifty-fifty mix of "qualified Coloured" and "you're-stuck-with-me Coloured."

I'm obviously joking here, but the reality is that these questions about my schooling and travel strip away the possibility for an authentic and meaningful connection by tossing me into one of two groups: "qualified" or not. And my interrogator's behavior toward me will then be based on that classification, not on the basis of whether or not I am actually capable of performing the work, have good character, am an interesting person, or anything else about me as a human being. It's all about categories.

Undeterred by this reality, I look for ways to respond to others on the basis of humanity, so that we might build a bridge between us. If a White South African asks me where I went to school, I remind myself that he may simply be curious and answer the question, following up by asking about his schooling because I am interested in learning about him as a unique human being. And if someone begins a conversation with a defensive comment such as "I had nothing to do with apartheid," I might ask in a neutral tone, "How do you feel about South African race relations today?" Their reply and the conversation that follows – if it follows – may reveal more about their underlying thoughts, unhappy feelings about what happened, and desire to connect with a Black person.

Sometimes the situation is different, and a White person feels she is being hit with the accusation of racism. When that happens, how can she turn what seems to be an accusatory conversation on racism into one based on humanity? Whites normally – and understandably – respond defensively, and the conversation spirals downward. Suppose, instead, that she responds with a comment that validates the other person's experience. For example, a White person accused of racism might say, "I know that Blacks historically, and through today, experience racism. I haven't had the experience; it must have been so hard." Saying this immediately validates the other person, and that often begins enabling bridging between the two of you.

There are no perfect words to say, and I sometimes pick the wrong ones. In every case, however, I aspire to enable bridging between two humans, even if I am feeling offended or fear that I have upset the other person beyond repair. That's because empathy – listening to the other person with an open heart and connecting with the person's feelings even if you don't agree – can put you in the other person's shoes, and that can often be a catalyst for repairing and strengthening broken, even hostile, relationships.

Irrespective of what race you are, empathy requires that we step away from judgment and our automatic responses, our knee-jerk defensiveness, anger, resentment, fear, or any of the other powerful emotions that can overwhelm us when the issue of race arises, especially if the accusations start flying. It means remembering that we are trying to bridge to the other person and that the emotions roiling between us are *not* the other person. It means remembering that it is often worthwhile exploring why that person is expressing these emotions, for the conversation that results may go a long way toward dissipating negative emotions and could possibly even turn them positive. The conversation may teach you a lot about the "other," and a lot about yourself as well.

Our Stories Inspire

My cousin Ruwaida Ismail is a nurse living and working in South Africa. Her mother, who is my mother's sister, is Coloured, but people thought she was White because she had fair skin, brown hair, and green eyes. Remember when I talked about how some of my grandfather's children looked White enough to visit him in the White-only hospital? She was one of them, though she was too young then to make the hospital visit.

Ruwaida's mother, my Aunt Shirley, married an Indian man. It had been a little difficult for them to date because she looked White, and under apartheid it was against the law for a White to marry an Indian. Since people looked askance at a "White" dating an Indian, they used an Indian friend as the "person in the middle," so people thought the two Indians were dating, not the Indian and the "White."

Ruwaida works in a fertility clinic. "I'm a midwife," she says, "so I birth babies. I give new life. As I see South Africa now, it has an entirely new life. It's as if a new birth has taken place, and we are nurturing the country so it will be healthy, strong, and beautiful, no matter what went on before. There are a lot of issues to work on, and there is a lot of blaming in the country, but South Africa is going to pull through."

I love how Ruwaida describes South Africa as having a new life with all the potential that new babies have. If I could choose one lesson for this new life to take to heart, it would be understanding the importance of building bridges between people. The simplest way to do so is to respond to each other with empathy, on the basis of humanity. That is, to listen to their story, recognize their struggle, and acknowledge their point of view.

Building bridges requires that we engage with others on the basis of humanity, even if we initially do so only as an act of faith. Then, as each bridge is built, we have the chance to connect with another person on the basis of our shared humanity, and to learn that the "other" is not a monolithic, irredeemable evil. I truly believe that when we reach out and interact with each other with open minds and hearts, we come to see each other as human beings rather than categories – and when we see each other as human beings, we can often work through our differences. In many cases, we can join hands and inspire others to do the same.

6

TRANSFORMING PAIN TO HEALING

I'VE SPOKEN A great deal about pain thus far, my pain and the pain of others.[14] Like many others, I first suppressed and then was forced to deal with lingering emotions – some of them, at least – and many of the wounds of apartheid and the poverty of my upbringing have scarred over. While my heart and actions are directed to bridging for authentic connections across race, I admit that residual pain remains, much of it stemming from what I perceive to be an ongoing lack of empathy from some White South Africans who, it seems, wish to wash their hands of the past. These people want nothing to do with the history that shaped me, despite the fact that it is our common history. At the same time, however, they continue to categorize me, and others, rather than to see and treat us as unique individuals. It seems as if they simultaneously wish to deny the racist past, and continue to use it as a lens through which to see others.

I had hoped for a "mirror" statement from a White South African, one speaking to the difficulty even a progressive White person eager for reconciliation might have with Blacks. But I was unable to obtain such a statement for, as it became apparent, many Whites are reluctant to speak of this openly or to go on record.

Many Whites were willing to speak about South Africa in general terms, saying that they were concerned about crime, corruption, and poor government service delivery. They also shared their fear of a perceived

---

14 While this chapter deals with pain, other aspects of restoration pivotal to reconciliation are discussed in chapters 9, 10, 11 and the Appendix.

dearth of future opportunities for their children. Beyond that, many Whites prefer to remain silent out of fear. "I have to work in South Africa," some have told me. "I can't afford to say anything." One White person expressed that in South Africa it feels that we are not moving forward because we are stuck in a narrative about race, we're caught in this old conversation loop that keeps us from moving forward.

While these responses to my queries provide some insight into the minds of Whites, they do not directly answer the question regarding any pain Whites may feel from the actions of Blacks, pain that hinders reconciliation. Could it be that they are afraid to admit that such pain exists? Could it be that there is not a space or forum where they would feel at ease to speak openly and frankly without fear of reprisal? Can one move from pain to healing if one is afraid to speak of the pain?

I believe we need a safe forum where the pain felt by all South Africans, Black and White, can be expressed, explored, and dealt with.

Embrace the Pain?
Apartheid and its lingering after-effects still pain the nation. And that is a frightening realization, for this pain stands in the way of racial reconciliation. Lack of reconciliation is a festering sore that hampers the social, economic, and other advances needed to propel South Africa into a prosperous, harmonious future.

We all feel pain, for we all are human. We all have reason to feel this pain, for we have all been wounded by someone or something. Some people quickly forgive those who, or that which, harmed them and move on. For them, pain is but a passing issue that does not become lingering anger. Other people do not realize they are in pain and, feeling only the resulting anger, have little opportunity to heal. Yet other people know they are in pain but do not recognize that they have the ability to deal with it. Instead, they focus on the person or group they feel has caused their agony and lash out in anger.

Sometimes it seems as if South Africa is awash in anger and violence, what with inequality, the feeling that there are no jobs, the frustration about poor service delivery, the cost of university education, issues related to land transfer without compensation, and so much more. Many are angry because they believe that certain jobs and neighborhoods are closed off to them and "their kind," and many harbor anger over the feeling that they and their group are being slighted.

Much of this is really pain manifesting as anger, an anger with roots that go back to what happened years before, and over things members of other groups say and do today. So much pain spews out as anger, and so often we fail to recognize the underlying hurt. The targets of this wrath certainly don't think about the underlying pain. Instead, they see the anger and the threat, to which they respond dismissively, defensively, or with an anger of their own. Individual pain levels ratchet up, as does the social pain level, and we sometimes seem to be locked in an endless, ever-more-frightening cycle of indignation, ire, or wrath.

I believe we would be much better off as individuals and as a society if we could recognize and deal with our pain before it becomes uncontrollable anger.

Healing at the Micro Level

I have spoken, directly or indirectly, about healing on the personal level in this book. For me, healing came through the process of working out my identity, realizing that I am so much more than a Coloured person as defined by apartheid, dealing with my lingering emotions, and experiencing gratefulness as I realized just how much support I received from my family and faith.

Talking about my pain with close confidants and family members, and putting it down on paper, was cathartic. In many cases, the act of speaking and being heard is all it takes to start the process of healing, so long as those to whom you are speaking listen to hear and not to judge. Talking in this manner doesn't always dispel your pain, but it certainly helps uncover hidden hurt, which you can then decide how to deal with. There are numerous ways to discover, explore, and process pain, ranging from two people informally coming together to share their stories and their pain, to broadly based, moderator-led group discussions guided by the essential principles of truth and reconciliation.

I encourage everyone to talk, and to listen with open ears and an open heart as the other person pours out her stories. I encourage everyone to create a space where stories and pain can be recounted and acknowledged, no matter how large or small that space may be, no matter who wishes to speak within it.

Healing at the Macro Level

Healing at the social and national level is just as important as healing at the personal level. In some ways, healing socially and nationally is more difficult, for it requires millions of people to make a deliberate effort to recognize, respond to, and release their pain, even the "righteous pain" that everyone agrees is justified because so many people did suffer in so many ways.

South Africa attempted to deal with its pain via – among other things – the Truth and Reconciliation Commission, a nation-wide effort to address the crimes perpetuated by apartheid, grant amnesty to the perpetrators in some cases, and call for rehabilitation and reparation where appropriate. The commission recorded the stories of those who had been falsely arrested, beaten, necklaced, or otherwise significantly harmed by or because of apartheid. It was an emotionally charged process, for it quite often brought victims in direct contact with their perpetrators. In some cases, however, it could do no more than acknowledge an incident.

Despite its limitations, the Commission was an excellent start. Can we take it further? A relatively small percentage of South Africans were included in the truth and reconciliation process. I hope this has brought them some measure of healing. And now, what of the rest, of the tens of millions of people denied a good education, shut out of many jobs, forced to live in crime-ridden slums far away from city centers, denied permission to use certain buses or dine in certain restaurants, and so much more? What of them and their pain? To what extent has their pain turned to anger? And to what extent is that anger hindering social healing and racial reconciliation?

What of those White South Africans who feel marginalized and occasionally vilified by the "all Whites are racist" outlook? What of those who fear that they or their children do not have a future in South Africa? What about their pain, fears, and potential anger?

Perhaps it's time to expand the truth and reconciliation concept, to inaugurate a nationwide effort to capture and address all of this pain, not just that which rose to the level of criminality or was a physical violation, beating, or detention. Imagine how healing it would be if tens of millions of South Africans were able to speak of the emotional pain they experienced during and after apartheid, and were truly heard.

I propose that South Africa initiate a "Phase Two" truth and reconciliation process that encourages groups of all types – from rural to township dwellers, from students to those who lack adequate levels of service – to air and discuss their concerns. All groups and communities, whether long-standing or ad hoc, whether well-established or newly self-aware, would be encouraged to participate. The individual members of all groups would be encouraged to do more than talk, and to get to know the "others" when possible – to eat with them; to visit their schools, neighborhoods, and even houses if possible; to walk that proverbial mile with someone unlike you with shoes exchanged in order to learn more about each other; to understand their concerns and recognize their humanity; and to publicly acknowledge that humanity. I believe this would be a giant leap forward.

In addition, organizations can set aside funds from their social investment or human resources budgets for staff to receive the professional counseling necessary to deal with residual pain, as well as any new emotions that may arise from issues in the organization pertaining to race relations. It will undoubtedly take some creative approaches to get people to truly open up and participate in frank discussions, no matter what side of an issue they may be on, but I believe that it is both possible and necessary.

Making Pain a Plus

Our ultimate goal should be to transform pain into a positive. Instead of a negative to be avoided, it should be a positive to be sought out. It should be exposed to the light, recognized, acknowledged, and empathized with.

When we see people acting out, rather than responding with disgust or anger, rather than throwing up the barricades, might we ask ourselves, "What is their pain?"

I believe that when a nation – any nation – commits itself to truly and honestly engaging with its members, and to affording opportunities for all to listen and discover their pains and needs, deep and permanent healing is possible. As the healing takes hold, the tide of racial reconciliation will follow, and we will be able to engage with each other authentically, on the basis of humanity. That is my hope.

PART TWO
BLAZING PATHWAYS TO WORLD-WIDE RECONCILIATION

7

PAIN IS A GLOBAL ISSUE

IN PART ONE I looked at my personal journey and suggestions for healing South Africa. Alas, my nation's pain is not unique, for countries all across the globe struggle with racial, ethnic, religious, class, and other forms of divide and strife. We can see how difficult these conflicts are to overcome by looking at the United States, where Blacks and Whites have only partially reconciled despite the fact that slavery was legally prohibited way back in 1865; despite the demise of apartheid-like "Jim Crow" restrictions in the 1960s.

Despite some strides forward, racial tensions remain and from time to time flare up. Susan Reed-Allen, a classmate of mine from the Harvard School of Government and a Black-American who has lived and worked in South Africa, has seen race relations play out in both countries. For her, the feeling of fatigue is a major issue:

I was born in Arkansas in 1964 and lived in Georgia and the D.C. area before moving to South Africa with my husband and our two sons. I think there's a major difference in the way the two countries have dealt with race relations and injustice. South Africa has owned it through the Truth and Reconciliation Process. No one denies apartheid, past racial injustices, or the residual disparities that have persisted until today. It happened and was wrong.

In the U.S., by contrast, there is still a fair number of people who feel that the United States has nothing to apologize for – even some who feel that the country did Black people a favor by bringing them to America. There is still a lot of denial around race relations in the U.S. Oftentimes, we would see questionable things happen, but we're always hit with an alternative explanation. If we attributed someone's words or actions to racial bias, we'd be told that we shouldn't be so quick to label it as racism. They just didn't want to acknowledge it.

Sometimes, even I didn't want to see it.

I remember when I was in junior high, I joined a YWCA-affiliated club called Y-Teens. We were a group of girls who met weekly with mentors to learn about things like life skills, arts, and culture. We also had slumber parties, dances, and other social events throughout the school year and attended camp for a week or two in the summer. For most of the time in the beginning, there were just two Black girls in the club. Interactions were fine, and we all got along well. Then, when I was in ninth grade, there was a push to grow the club's membership. In a short time, the dynamic of the group changed as more Black students joined to the point where the White girls were in the minority. We had been meeting after school in one of the art classrooms, which was convenient for everyone. At the beginning of the next school year, it was announced that meetings would move to the homes of a few of the White girls, mostly located in exclusive White communities, and be held in the evenings as opposed to immediately after school. Most of the White girls either lived in these communities or had cars or friends with cars. Most of the Black girls did not and ultimately dropped out of the club.

Even at the young age of fifteen or so, this really bothered me. On one level, I saw what was happening, but I didn't want to "get it" because all this time, I'd considered these girls to be my friends. Finally, I had to accept it for what it was, and I stopped participating.

A year or so later, a group of these girls approached me and basically said, "We miss you – come back." I was really touched and decided to give it another try. So I and the young lady I'd started out with rejoined the club. The group was all White again except for the two of us. At the first meeting we attended, the girls talked about calendars featuring cute guys on campus that they were selling to raise money for planned social activities. There were three Black guys in the calendar. It quickly became clear that the White girls wanted the two Black girls to "cover" the Black community, to sell the calendar to the Blacks. They didn't want me back in Y-Teens; they wanted my skin color.

You might say, "That was decades ago; things are different." Are they? Just a few years ago, my son, then a student at Morehouse College in Atlanta, was stopped by the police while driving. The reason why he was stopped kept changing. My son was a university student, very well-spoken and clean-cut, polite, and pretty conservative in his appearance, yet the officer, who was White, still stopped and detained him for dubious reasons. He claimed there was a warrant, treated him like a criminal, and was preparing to take him to jail! Because my husband and I were thousands of miles away in South Africa, our son called his uncle, who straightened things out. Ultimately, my son was released without being charged with the alleged issues he was initially stopped for.

My son was violated and traumatized – for what? Most likely for being a young, Black male driving a nice car. He was so embarrassed that he didn't fully share the incident with us for some time. When he finally did, I was immediately reminded of something similar that happened to my husband and me when we lived in Georgia.

My husband, myself, and our two small sons were driving through a predominantly White county in Georgia on our way home to spend Christmas with family. When our toddler needed a potty break, we took the next exit with a gas station/convenience store. It was well after midnight and very dark. There were no other cars on the road in that area. My husband turned onto the main road and proceeded to the gas station. Almost immediately, a patrol car pulled into the parking lot behind us with blue lights flashing. A white female officer approached our car and told my husband he'd made an illegal right turn on red. As he began explaining that he hadn't noticed the sign, I got out to take my son inside. I was perfectly comfortable leaving my husband alone with the officer: Why wouldn't I be? Later, when I exited the store, I saw that there were two additional cruisers behind our car, also with lights flashing, and my husband – still seated in the vehicle – was surrounded by several White police officers.

The initial officer had called for backup and was berating my husband while her colleagues stood closely by in an intimidating show of force. She looked and sounded so angry, acting like we had just committed some horrible offense. It would have been funny were it not so unsettling. My husband, who is a minister, is about the most inoffensive-looking and unassuming person you can imagine. He was trying to explain that our young child needed to go to the bathroom and apologized for the infraction. He complied with the customary request for license and registration, but nothing seemed to satisfy these cops. He tried to lighten the mood by pointing out the obvious – that we were on a holiday road trip in a car filled with babies and presents. That we were traveling at night so that the kids would sleep most of the way. But this officer, who seemed determined to drag out the process, kept lecturing him. It was like she wanted to escalate the situation.

Finally I said, "You know what? We're driving home for Christmas, we still have a long way to go, so write the ticket and we'll be on our way." It took more time, but she gave us the ticket and let us drive off – then followed us for several miles on the interstate.

In most cases, you just pay the ticket and forget about it. But my husband was so impacted by what happened that night that he drove back to that county several weeks later for his court date. He recounted the whole story to the judge, telling him, "I'm very offended. I was going home for Christmas with my wife and small children in the car. Yes, I made an illegal turn, I'm not disputing that. But the response from the officers was disproportionate."

The judge apologized to my husband and dismissed the

ticket.

In the small town in Arkansas where my husband and I are from, a lot of people have police scanners in their houses. I don't know why, but they do. I often visit one of my relatives while my husband takes the car and goes to visit his family and old friends. It hardly fails that while he is moving about the town, we hear repeated mentions on the scanner of our family car – running the license plates over and over, checking for outstanding warrants for the registered owner. It became a source of entertainment. We could literally track my husband's movements by the police chatter.

I can't prove that any of these things happened because of race, but each is another in a long series of incidents like this, going back generations in my family. When my father wanted to buy a house in an all-White neighborhood, his loan paperwork was mysteriously delayed until the deal fell through – however, the loan was approved immediately afterwards when it was too late because the offer to purchase had expired. I worked in banking back then, so I knew there was something odd about the way the transaction played out.

All the mysterious things like that. All the police stops. All the times people have said things like, "We like you, but we don't like the other people like you." All the times people at school and work have said things in my presence because they felt I wasn't one of "those Blacks" and would understand. All the things like this that pile up, and we're told to excuse them. We're told that we're misunderstanding and overthinking. That we're seeing racism where there is none. Any one, or two, or ten of them could be misunderstandings, but not all of them.

I like to give everybody the benefit of the doubt, but how many times do we have to? How many times do we try to convince people that we're OK, that we're worthy?

We are well aware of the assumptions people make about Blacks. We may try to assimilate, we may strip ourselves of our Blackness, strip ourselves of our culture, strip ourselves of our speech because something about us makes others uncomfortable. And yet with all of this yielding and morphing, the assumptions persist. In the past ten years or so, I've decided I'm not so concerned with making people feel comfortable with me. I am different. I don't want to hear, "Susan, despite your color. . ." because that implies there's something wrong with my color. I love my color. I want you to see my color yet not have it make you think less of me.

We're always the ones who have to reach across the aisle to convince others that we're relevant and human. I'm just so tired of it all. This fatigue is widespread in the Black community, and we are at a loss for what to do. Some react with anger and bitterness, some stick their heads in the sand and don't think about it. But it's there. And in America, we don't seem to know how to deal with it, how to even talk about it.

Susan is very aware of her emotions and of how they bleed into her everyday thinking. So is Jay, a White American man who freely admits that he is hesitant to interact with Black-Americans. Jay, who is Jewish, was raised in Los Angeles at a time when the city was still emerging from the era of "redlining," the unofficial policy practiced by real estate agents and banks to only show houses and make loans to certain people in certain areas. They would literally draw red lines on their office maps to indicate which area "belonged" to which group. Most of the "others," which in days not too far past included the Jews, were relegated to outlying areas such as the Boyle Heights neighborhood, which had once been heavily Jewish. When the Jews gained acceptance in the 1950s they moved out to "regular" neighborhoods, and Boyle Heights became largely Hispanic.

Jay's family moved to an area that was White but becoming heavily Asian and was adjacent to a Hispanic area. His father, a medical doctor, happened to work with many Hispanic doctors and treat Hispanic patients. "I had lots of interactions with Asians and Hispanics when I was little," Jay says. "I went to elementary school with Asians and played baseball with them at the park. But not with the Hispanics; they lived a neighborhood over. However, from the time I was four or five, my father would sometimes take me on nighttime house calls. We'd go into houses in Hispanic neighborhoods, and there was always a grandmother who would take one look at me and say, 'You're so skinny!' She'd say it in Spanish, which I don't speak, but I understood because that's what every grandmother said when they saw me. Jewish, Asian, Hispanic, it didn't matter – every grandmother thought I was too skinny. She'd take me in the kitchen and give me milk and cookies while my father took care of the patient."

Jay's family later moved to an all-White and largely Jewish neighborhood, but his family continued to interact with the Hispanic doctors and their families and other Hispanics they met through them. "I have a mental database filled with experiences with Asians and Hispanics," Jay says. "Almost all of them good. So if I have a bad experience today, it is easily balanced by all those good experiences."

But the situation is entirely different with respect to Blacks. "We barely even saw Blacks when I was growing up. All I knew about them was what I saw on TV or read in the newspapers, which was rarely good." This was in the 1960s, an era of sometimes violent civil rights protests in the United States, so Jay saw and read about Black "agitators" and "looters" and "rioters," and saw Blacks in mostly negative or subservient roles on television. "I have this powerful mental image of Blacks being in your face all the time. Threatening, violent. My family is liberal and in favor of equal rights and equal opportunity. My parents were constantly sponsoring Hispanics, helping them get jobs so they could get their green cards. And my mom was the representative for a Korean orphanage, helping to arrange for Koreans in Los Angeles to adopt babies from Korea. She did this for free. We used to go to these picnics in the park, where all the Korean families who had adopted a baby through my mother would come with all their children. And we wound up adopting a Korean orphan. I feel very comfortable meeting and interacting with Asians, Hispanics, Indians, or anyone else. Except Blacks. Unless it's a business situation, or a friend is introducing me, I hold back a little, waiting for an indication of how they will respond."

Although Jay went to a liberal college, there were relatively few Black students, and they largely kept to their own. "Most of the Blacks sat at their own table in the dining hall. I'd look at that table and think I should go over and introduce myself but then think, 'No. I won't be welcomed.' I went to some speeches and meetings on race relations, but they always seemed eager to recount all the terrible things Whites were and still are."

Jay's career trajectory kept him working with Whites, Hispanics, and others, but he worked with only the occasional Black. He lived in mostly White neighborhoods with small numbers of Asians, Hispanics, and others, but there were hardly any Blacks. "For decades, almost all my experience with Blacks was on the news, and it was almost always negative. I remember a couple of Blacks who were often on the news, perpetually angry with the Whites, always accusing and insisting that Whites were horrible and responsible for all their ills."

In his mid-thirties, Jay was working as an executive at small firm and went to a seminar to learn about the latest laws regarding fair play in the workplace. "I was looking forward to it because I really wanted to make sure we were treating everyone properly, but what I learned was unsettling. I learned that if a minority, particularly a Black, said you crossed some line, you were in big trouble. The instructors were very clear about this, and I asked questions to make sure I understood. All it took was for someone to file a complaint with the government, and you were assumed guilty until proven otherwise. You might be in for years of litigation, and even if you proved the accusation was complete nonsense, you could be wiped out because you had to pay your lawyers. Do you know what my take-away lesson was? Think very carefully before hiring another Black person."

To this day, Jay is cautious about interacting with Blacks. He's had some good experiences with Blacks as well as some bad experiences, such as the time he was walking down the street and a Black person shouted something about "the Whites like you!" at him. Another time, when he asked a Black man at the gym to turn down his music, he was verbally assaulted.

> *Some Blacks feel that Whites should bear "White guilt" and that we should accept responsibility for what our ancestors did to theirs. Well, while their ancestors were being forced to work as slaves down South, mine were being beaten and raped by Cossacks or forcibly impressed into the Russian army at the age of twelve and held there for twenty-five years. While their*

parents were being taught to be especially careful and respectful when dealing with Whites, mine were being beaten up by the neighborhood kids who didn't like "kikes" and "Christ-killers." Especially on Easter – that was the favorite time for the Catholic boys to swarm into the Jewish neighborhoods in Philadelphia and New Jersey where my parents grew up and beat the Jewish kids. While their parents were being denied entry to White colleges, my father was asked to trace his family history on certain college applications, for these schools didn't want too many undesirables, which back then included Jews. And while their fathers were being denied jobs by Whites, my father was quietly barred from practicing medicine at certain hospitals in Los Angeles because they already had a Jew or two on staff, and as everyone knew back then, "Two Jews is plenty."

I understand the pain of being the "other," at least historically speaking, for my family was oppressed in Europe as far back as we can trace. I only exist because my grandparents fled Europe and were not slaughtered during the Holocaust, as was just about all of my family that remained behind.

I fully understand that I've benefited from a system that accords Whites privileges, even if it was just a generation before mine that Jews were finally allowed in. I also fully understand that my view of Blacks is skewed by the presentation of Blacks in the media. But then I look at the media today, and I'm still hearing Whites being blamed.

I'm happy to interact with anyone. But I don't want to be seen as "the White guy" who bears responsibility for their travails, who should sit there quietly and absorb their anger, who should be lectured on racism and privilege. I want them to see me for who I am and like me or dislike me because of me, not because they look at my skin color and decide that I fit some stereotype.

I have a friend, an Arab Muslim who ran a Muslim-Jewish dialogue group. He says, when speaking to the "other," that there's a field between us, and let's meet halfway. I'm happy to meet anyone halfway, three-quarters of the way, even all the

> *way over on their side. I just want to know that when I get there, I'll be seen as me, a guy named Jay. That's what I am: a guy named Jay who happens to be White.*

Susan and Jay's stories speak to the terrible damage that can be done when negative experiences trigger negative emotions that seep into your thinking. Both want to be accepted for who they are and not be treated badly because of skin color. Yet, it seems as if they're standing on opposite ends of that field, disheartened by each other's race group. I know both Susan and Jay. I believe that despite the past and negative experiences, they can find the deeper humility and grace required to give each other a chance, to listen and connect with each other. I hope that they and all the other Susans and Jays of the world can take baby steps toward each other and, with time, meet in the middle.

Many well-intentioned people on opposite sides of the divide – any divide, be it racial, ethnic, religious, class, or other – find it impossible to take meaningful steps toward each other. As you'll see in the next chapter, people from different parts of the world have distinct ideas about reconciliation, what it means and how to achieve it, and even those who genuinely wish to "meet in the middle" can find it difficult, if not impossible, to do so. Others, fortunately, have found ways to do so.

My hope is that one day, in the not-too-distant future, the field that still separates many of us will become our shared space for healing and positive emotions, and we will walk it together.

8

DIFFERENT PATHS TO RECONCILIATION

I CANNOT LIVE with resentment, anger and hatred, whether it is my own or claimed by others. For me, reconciliation is a vital part of the response to apartheid and the many other horrors perpetrated by one group upon another. You may disagree, you may prefer retribution only, but I cannot live with a burning hole in my heart. I *must* heal, and to heal I must forgive, and I must try to keep an open mind and heart towards those hailing from groups which have harmed me.

For me, the journey from hurt to handshake has included reflection, grappling with forgiveness, and addressing my feelings of pain, vulnerability, and other lingering emotions. It has included learning as much about myself as possible, which has made me realize how connected I am to "others" all around the world, including some who have harmed me and mine. And the journey has involved listening to the stories of others.

I have found a great deal of inspiration in listening to the stories of others from around the world who have been harmed. Sometimes, we become totally absorbed in our individual oppression; we feel that no one has been harmed as we have, no one understands what we have endured, and no one can possibly show us a way forward. Feeling that way is natural, but it is isolating. It sets us aside from all others, it becomes a barrier to moving forward. I have found that listening to the stories of others increases my connection to humanity and to the common struggles we face. Further, it improves my perspective. And listening to the stories of others heartens and strengthens me, for I am inspired by the incredible bravery they showed in enduring and overcoming.

On the flip side, I also gain perspective and move further toward reconciliation by hearing the stories of people from the groups who oppressed others.

I can't prescribe the path to reconciliation, for it depends on the individual and the situation. I can, however, offer the stories of some of my friends and colleagues, along with their perspectives on reaching out. I hope you will find as much inspiration in these stories as I have. While there is no single answer contained in these stories, I can assure you there is endless inspiration.

"It's More Acceptance"

I met Huguette Umutoni in Geneva, Switzerland, where we were colleagues at the World Economic Forum. She's quite accomplished, having earned a Bachelor's Degree in Peace Studies and International Relations in the United Kingdom, then a Master's Degree in International Negotiation and Policy Making at the Graduate Institute of International Studies in Geneva. She's also wonderfully warm and loving, a life-of-the-party person who makes everyone feel welcome. Upon first meeting her, it's hard to imagine the horror she experienced as a very young girl. And it's easy to understand why she wonders if reconciliation is even possible. Here's her story, in her words:

> *I was eight years old when the Rwandan genocide began, and ended, leaving behind as many as one million dead Tutsis, many of them literally hacked to death with machetes by their neighbors. By people they had called friends and invited into their homes to share a meal.*
>
> *My family was among the "lucky ones," the two thousand and fifty or so people hiding in a church called Saint Paul; men, women, and children protected by a priest, Father Celestin. The fact that he was able to protect us for so long – until the 17th of June, when we were rescued by Rwandan Patriotic Front (RPF) – was amazing.*

The Genocide against the Tutsi in Rwanda started when the majority Hutus decided to eradicate the minority Tutsis in 1994. My mother, siblings, some of my cousins and I hid at Saint Paul. A Hutu militia, approximately twelve men, sometimes more, came several times to kill us but Father Celestin would always find something to give them, sometimes beer, sometimes money, and they would go away. But they always came back, sometimes the next day, sometimes two or three days later.

The fact that Father Celestin was able to keep them at bay, at least for a while, was lifesaving. And the fact that he was willing to do so was amazing for he was also Hutu, yet he was risking his own life to save ours.

The militia was a constant threat, a sword waiting to fall on our heads. Sometimes they would come and see what you were wearing. If you were wearing too many clothes they would say you were a spy and kill you, or take you away with them for torture.

The militia would take people, have them dig their own holes and then kill them. One day we were hiding in a kind of a bunker and right next to me was an old man who had died in the crossfire. I have many such memories and I have heard many more stories like that; so many that I've had to numb my mind to keep my sanity. Sometimes those images come back to me. So does the question: How can people who were your neighbors or whom you employed, trusted, and sometimes even loved, how can they come and look at you like you don't matter anymore? I remember the day a group of militia came and entered the room. Among them was this guy who used to look after our house and I remember him not looking at us straight in the eyes, I could feel his shame. One could tell that he was accepting the orders he had been given, shouting loudly and even proudly saying, "Look at you, you will soon be dead!"

Another day, a different group of militia came and took the women, including my mother. My little sister was four and my brother was two at the time. As they were taking the women away, my mother told me that since I was the oldest,

I would have to grow up real fast and look after my siblings. I understood then that there was a possibility that I might not see her again. We couldn't cry in those times, we just watched by and accepted situations.

An hour later, all the women came back. They were alive, but it's not hard to imagine what could have happened to them during that hour. But we never talked about it.

Finally, the day came when a bigger group of militia decided it was time for us to die. The day before our death, they came and said "We're not going to forgive you this time, no bribe will save you. We're going to kill all of you, starting from the little baby to the oldest among you."

We began to mentally prepare ourselves to die. We were praying a lot, embracing the life we had and waiting to die. Then, at 3 am, we heard that the Rwandan Patriotic Front (RPF) had come – they were the Tutsi army that would save us. However, amongst all the chaos, we weren't sure if it was the right group or not, and we didn't want to die running. We wanted to make sure it wasn't the Hutus playing games with us. Eventually, we somehow realized it was the RPF and grew very excited.

People started running, everywhere. I found myself alone, I couldn't find my mum, aunt, cousins, my brother or sister. With no more strength to go on, I sat on the floor. I sat there and waited for them to come and kill me. A woman, who was my parents' friend, came to me and lied to me. She took my hand and, to get me to follow her, said, "I saw your parents, they are looking for you everywhere. Let's go." I got up and we started running.

It was pitch dark, approximately 4 am, and it was as if bad luck was following us. We took a wrong turn and found ourselves in the middle of the Hutu militias. We had to improvise; we told them that we had come to warn them about the RPF and the many Tutsi who were escaping. We then turned back, hurried away and I honestly do not remember how we found ourselves with the right group and joined the queue, rescued. It took us a full day to finally be in a safe place, and another day to be in an area fully controlled by the RPF, where we could sit and eat.

At one point we stopped to wait for some people to catch up with us and it was then that I saw my dad. He was shot in his leg. I hadn't seen him for a month and a half; I thought he was dead. As we continued to the safe place the RPF had secured for us, I didn't let go of his hand.

A month later, in July, my life restarted, it began returning to its course. We resettled in new homes, we lived with various members of our families for the first few months, and we told each other stories of the Genocide.

My dad had a harder time than us because he wanted to leave Rwanda, he felt like there was no purpose for him to stay and rebuild his life in Kigali. He told mum, "Let's just leave the country and rebuild it in Uganda." But my mom didn't want to leave. And both my parents wanted to find their parents. It was their mission, for one of the key ways to let go of what happened was to find your lost ones and bury their bones – or at least learn where they were killed, and how.

Looking back, I realize that I put what happened in my brain and forgot about it. I don't think there's anything we can call closure regarding Rwanda. For many people, like my parents, the way to have some closure is to be "lucky" and find who murdered your loved ones. They may tell you where to find them in order for you to bury them with dignity. Personally, I didn't have any hatred, but it changed my personality. I over-compensate by being too nice, by not allowing myself to be sad. I think I try too much to be rational.

I don't know if I believe in reconciliation – it's more acceptance, and it becomes normal with time. I learned to accept what happened and then move forward for my own sake. I have managed to bury my anger and sadness caused by those many losses, and one can only take one step forward at a time. This takes time; probably a whole generation, or my children's children! Even then, the memories will linger.

In Huguette's story I see so much pain and suffering, yet the

Huguette I know is so full of joy and love. Her response to the terrible suffering that she, her family, ethnic group, and entire nation endured reminds me to cultivate joy and thankfulness.

I Do Not Believe There Can Be Reconciliation Yet

Tshering is a dear friend whom I met through the Young Global Leaders. I visited him in Kathmandu and had the heartwarming experience of Tshering taking me to his rural village and the very house he was raised in. The village needs much repair following the 2015 Nepal earthquake and I am inspired by Tshering's passion and actions to restore it.

I am a Hyolmo, an indigenous people of Nepal, born in a mountain village in Nepal called Sermathang, in Helambu region. I lived in the same modest house until the age of seventeen; we were seven people living in the house with no private or separate rooms.

There are not many Hyolmo people in Nepal. The population estimates are uncertain, ranging from several thousand to perhaps eighty thousand out of a total population of about twenty-nine million. We live in the hilly regions, where we practice our traditional lifestyle, with our own language and customs. We are taught how interdependent we are, and that we should respect and be there for each other. For example, during someone's funeral or memorial service, the villagers make rice, fire-wood, financial and other contributions. Furthermore, each household has certain responsibilities to perform at village ceremonies and celebrations.

Unfortunately, our indigenous culture has always been overshadowed by the majority of Nepal, and there remains a great deal of discrimination in the country. The caste system heavily influences ranking in society, and we don't fit into a rank anywhere on the caste system.

One of the many ways in which the Hyolmo and other indigenous people are discriminated against is with access to education and other government services. Our village had one government school but it only went up to grade seven and, in any case, most public schools did not function well. After grade seven, the nearest school was far away, so many children did not continue. I am fortunate to have been part of the first batch to complete full schooling in the village, in a school started by an Indian (from Darjeeling) teacher to offer English-based education. Later, secondary school education was added on. However, I wished for more and moved to Kathmandu after graduating high school to complete my A levels.[15]

The first time I travelled to Kathmandu, at the age of seventeen, it took four hours of walking down the hill, traversing a rough road, and a further five hours to Kathmandu. Moving to Kathmandu was a culture shock. In the village you can live by a barter system and the culture systems are humane, they are about how you share with each other. Kathmandu is way more individualistic.

But I was eager to learn. Also, I was volunteering at a children's hospital as I wanted to understand health, which would better equip me to help my community, where healthcare is sorely lacking. I then moved to England to pursue higher education, becoming the first person from the Hyolmo ethnic group to earn a Ph.D. (in Telemedicine). This shows that everyone has the potential, as long as one is given the opportunity. Education has given me freedom, exposure to the world, and a sense of responsibility. Education is a big part of my journey and helped me overcome discrimination. My Ph.D. from a United Kingdom university has enabled me to interact with anyone and to be treated as an equal.

Discrimination is systemic in Nepal. The government barely wishes to acknowledge us: remember, we don't rank anywhere on the caste system. For example, when the first census was done in Nepal, the officials who came to my village felt that everyone looked the same, so they decided to call us all

---

15 A Levels are advanced courses required for admission to university in the United Kingdom and certain other countries.

"Lama." Everyone in my village has the surname of Lama.

You can also see discrimination with the schools, which are inadequate in the villages. It's as if the government wants us to remain uneducated, so we cannot learn how the system works and how to speak up for ourselves. The lack of schooling is harder on girls than it is on boys, for after seventh grade most girls either get married or take on expanded household tasks for their own families. Tragically, many girls were and continue to be trafficked, sold to brothels in India and elsewhere.

Immediately after the Nepal earthquake of 2015, sex trafficking increased as people lost their homes and schools and, in many cases, their parents. So after the earthquake we began building schools and community centers. This is another level of systematic discrimination: not being on the government's priority list for rebuilding the villages and infrastructure.

I am also working towards re-building the village, for without our village, we have no identity. The village has given me identity, so I want to make sure the dignity of the Hyolmo people is restored.

Reconciliation between the many groups is needed, but the people and system that discriminated against us may not be ready. I honestly do not believe there can be reconciliation in Nepal while discrimination is so deeply rooted, and linked to centuries of religious and cultural practices. Yes, the monarchy was abolished in 2008 and Hinduism is no longer the state religion – we are a secular republic. This is a step forward, but it will be very difficult to eradicate deep-rooted discrimination, so quick reconciliation is not possible.

Reconciliation is about self-awareness and reflection and independence. It is about being aware of the problems, and having a place where people can express how sorry they are for acts of discrimination. I cannot see any of this happening any time soon. But if we cannot reconcile, we can bring people together and unify around a common cause, working together even while we celebrate our diversity. We can rally around what we have in common rather than focusing on our differences. I was able to get the government, senior ministers, and people from different walks of life involved in projects such as Childreach Nepal, and our new initiative, IdeaStudio, a platform to support Nepalese with promising social business ideas.

It will take a long time for equality, an end to discrimination, and the beginning of the reconciliation process. I see reconciliation in Nepal as a gradual and evolving process of acceptance of different cultures and castes – presently, there are some marriages across castes, which before was unthinkable. I myself went against the grain of my ethnic tribe and married a Vietnamese woman.

While reconciliation will take much time, it is positive that the wheels are slowly turning.

Upon reading Tshering's story, I feel both despair and hope. Despair because he feels that reconciliation is impossible for now, and hope because he has found ways to improve life for his village, his ethnic group, children, and the nation as a whole.

You Can't Hate Whole Categories of People

My dynamic friend Lara Setrakian is an Armenian-American whose great-grandparents survived the brutal Armenian Genocide, which saw as many as one-and-a-half million Armenians slaughtered at the hand of the Turkish government in 1915 and 1917. Lara is the very embodiment of the American immigrant success story, for she graduated from Harvard University, carved out a successful career in the media, and founded News Deeply, "an innovative network of theme-driven information and community platforms, convening engaged, knowledgeable and passionate audiences." It's interesting that the company she created is so fiercely dedicated to understanding the truth, because for Lara, reconciliation began with the realization that while some Turks behaved atrociously, others did not. In fact, some of them extended a hand in friendship, even at risk to themselves. Here's her story, in her words:

For thousands and thousands of years, my family lived within a narrow band that's now Eastern Turkey. That all came to an end in 1915, and we moved wherever we could find safety. In the search for home many of us landed in Syria and Lebanon but then, with the start of the Lebanese Civil War in 1975, my parents fled to the U.S.

I know the stories, I understand how difficult it was for them to be displaced, to lose their land and leave their culture behind. The dislocation has led to one hundred years of trauma and pain, which has left us feeling quite diminished. I grew up in a community that was so aware of that.

I spent a lifetime working through a lot of difficult emotions: anger, confusion, with a lot of pain at the heart of it all. Not understanding why someone would come after someone like me based on who I am, or what religion I follow. It took me a long time to figure it out, beginning when I traveled back to Turkey in 2012. I was invited there for a conference on the Arab Spring – I was the first person in my family to be invited there since we fled – to the very town my mother came from. It took me through the looking glass to the other side, and it changed my life. I felt a reconnect to the land and people. I made friends with Turks who might have been my neighbors, whose families might have known my family.

I saw the house where my great-great uncle lived, the church where my family prayed. I wasn't angry; I was grateful that I had the chance to see it. I had new Turkish friends who stopped everything to show me around, who really respected the fact that I was a granddaughter of this town who came home to visit.

Diplomats talk about normalizing relations – but normalizing is not just for countries, it's for people. I was becoming normalized. It was such a gift, it was magical, a huge part of my personal healing. Up close in Turkey, I could understand that the truth was that some people were the perpetrators of terrible things – some, not all. Some people let their greed and fear trump any humanity or sense of kinship, and made very bad decisions. In the town I came from, they didn't hate us; they loved us. In fact, some Armenians left their children behind with the Turkish neighbors to care for them because they trusted their neighbors more than they trusted what would happen on the road. On my father's side, our Turkish friends and neighbors helped us get away to safety. When Armenians were no longer allowed to sell their property, these friends and neighbors sold it for us and sent us the proceeds to help us get started somewhere else.

You can't hate whole categories of people: it's not a whole category of people who made that decision. There were a whole lot of Turkish people who loved my ancestors. Realizing this was a game-changer.

My life had been shaped by the genocide. I have workaholic tendencies that come from that trauma, from the sense that success could protect you. That if you were well-regarded enough, people would help you; that if you had money stashed in your mattress you might survive.

I no longer define myself by the tragedy, but through the great legacy of the culture and religion and music that survives. Through the legacy of our thousands of years of Armenian culture. Through the good things that remain.

Everyone has their own way of processing pain. I've decided that I'm not interested in remaining angry. I'm interested in concrete, restorative justice. For example, there is a movement to get Turkey to give back the churches to the Armenian community. What could be more just? I feel it's my job to be engaged in a community-wide conversation about the way forward.

In Lara's story I recognize one of my own unconscious responses to suffering. She speaks of how she over-compensated with success, believing that success was insurance against poverty. I realize that I had done the same thing.

Let's Talk

Denise Velasco, who was my classmate in the master's program at Harvard Kennedy School of Government, was born in Los Angeles to Mexican immigrants. She moved to Orange County when she was seven years old, where hers was the first Mexican family in the neighborhood. There was some backlash from neighbors, with one saying the presence of Denise's family would "bring down the family values in the neighborhood." Denise's experiences with discrimination fueled her passion for a career in activism and social justice, and she has dedicated her life to social justice. Upon graduating from U.C. Berkeley, Denise worked for Justice for Janitors for five years in Los Angeles and Orange County, and currently serves as Labor Relations Representative for the Orange County Employees Association.

In a recent conversation, Denise touched upon the subject of reconciliation when she talked about how we think we're different from others, but at heart, we're all quite similar. Indeed, we may even share blood and history with the ones we think are so dissimilar. If we would embrace that reality, and put our hearts into talking about the difficult subjects we tend to avoid, we could solve many of the issues that divide us.

> *When looking at others, people are often not seeing the whole picture. If they would look closely, they would understand we all have the same troubles, concerns, and feelings, the same need for love and compassion.*
>
> *We're not understanding how interconnected we are, even when we think we're distinctly a member of this group or of that group. My family is from Mexico, and along the northern border of Mexico you'll find a Chinese population – they couldn't get into the U.S. during the period when Chinese were barred, so they settled in Mexico. Along the coastal areas of Mexico you'll find a strong African influence, which has to do with slavery. Studies say the African blood content in the Mexican population rivals the indigenous content. There are the indigenous people in Mexico, hundreds of tribes. We also have the European influence from Spain and Italy – when there is war and famine, or opportunity, people travel.*
>
> *Talk about an intersection of history and peoples in one country! And at the end of the day, everyone is trying to do the best they can to advance their families.*

We need to start talking to each other, talking about the difficult subjects we've tried to stay away from. People tend to scream at each other, not listen to each other. I don't like to avoid things, I want to take things on. Let's begin to address conflict head on, let's stop avoiding the uncomfortable conversations. If you go through conflict in a healthy way, you always see an advance in understanding – even if the understanding is that we completely disagree and have to dissolve the relationship.

Denise's view was echoed in a recent conversation I had with Mosharraf Zaidi, a noted Pakistani columnist who advises international organizations and governments on aid and public policy. Born in Canada, Mosharraf spent time as a child in Pakistan, moving there again at the age of sixteen.

I grew up with great sense of intimacy and brotherhood toward fellow Muslims and a sense of Muslim victimhood, particularly with respect toward Palestine and Kashmir.[16] So my natural posture towards India was informed by this grievance. When I moved to Pakistan my grievance was exacerbated because the Pakistani state actively cultivates the grievance, and had been involved in armed conflict with India multiple times. This was my view throughout my teens and early twenties.

The 2008 Mumbai terrorist attacks were a turning point for Mosharraf. This first, live telecast terrorist attack saw members of a UN-sanctioned militant organization, based in Pakistan, bombing and shooting up a dozen targets over the course of four days in the Indian city of Mumbai, including a hospital, cinema, railway station, hotel, restaurant, and Jewish community center.

It was a stark moment for Mosharraf, who felt that Indians needed to hear from Pakistanis how outraged they were by this terrorist attack. There was such an accumulation of injury and counter-injury, grievance and counter-grievance; it had piled high over the decades since Pakistan was split off from India, and over the centuries

---

16 Kashmir is the northernmost portion of the Indian subcontinent. Control over the area and its inhabitants has long been disputed, with pieces of it currently being held by Pakistan, India, and China.

of religious conflict between Muslims, Hindus, and others in the subcontinent. Horrific as the Mumbai attacks were, they fit the pattern of what had been happening since before anyone could remember. And now something had to change.

> *Pakistanis and Indians needed to feel a joint sense of injury caused by all this conflict. If they could share a sense of injury, as opposed to continually inflicting injury on each other, we could heal the wounds. In grade six, in Canada, my best friend was an Indian boy named Manish. I knew he was Indian and Hindu, but did not think I was crossing a major barrier by being his friend. Yet, while I hated what India did to Kashmir, I loved Manish. I could always interact with Indians at the human level. I couldn't dehumanize Indians, even as we were in dispute, because I had met and personally known Indians.*

In the decade since the Mumbai attack, Mosharraf has participated in multiple "track two" initiatives – these are discussions of various issues between non-official representatives of the various sides. His high-level experience has taught him that progress is achievable, and that progress is vulnerable: all it takes is one incident or one poorly worded press release to restart conflict. That's why he feels it is so very important to talk, and to keep talking.

> *I fear that if we do not have an ongoing conversation between a critical mass of Indians and Pakistanis a bad situation can get worse, and a worse situation can become extreme with no resistance. The foundational substance of resistance comes from the availability of a critical mass of champions who engage with each other whilst representing the views prevalent in their own countries, and also act as ambassadors of the other country within their own context. So, if we have a critical mass of people who can sustain the process of reconciliation, we can absorb some of the anger when a conflict re-ignites.*

> *So, we need to never stop talking. The angrier we are with each other, the more we need to talk. Not talking, or terrorism, or war, is not the answer. We need to talk to each other with a consciousness that there is spectacular evil in the air – all the time. We need to talk. Not because of it, but in spite of it.*

Both Denise and Mosharraf, coming from very different backgrounds, emphasize the importance of talking with the "other."

Fears Are Real, but Not Insurmountable
I met Katherine Graham when we were twenty-something and acting in a play together at our church, which had a diverse congregation. This church placed a great deal of importance on diversity, holding sessions on reconciliation and making sure people were greeted at the beginning of each service in their many languages. I liked Katherine instantly as our arty sides connected and Katherine is very thoughtful, and open to all people. Katherine is a writer who lives in Cape Town, South Africa. She and her husband have two sons and have just adopted a Black daughter.

> *I think I was about five when I first became aware of my whiteness. Or rather, I became aware that there were others around me who didn't look like me. Growing up in Durban, I remember my parents chuckling under their breath when I greeted an Indian with a hearty, "Sawubona!" I didn't realize then that Indians didn't speak Zulu. Even then at that age, I was making a clumsy attempt to bridge the gap between myself and others who were different from me the only way I knew how – through language.*
>
> *That pursuit continued into my teens and twenties. As a junior TV reporter, I cashed in my unit trusts to study Zulu. I was thrilled when Jesmane invited me to visit her home in Westbury, Johannesburg, allowing me to glimpse her reality of growing up in a Coloured community. Now that I've moved to the Western Cape, I've picked up some Xhosa and enjoy practicing the few phrases I know with petrol attendants and shop assistants. I'm fortunate that through our local church, my husband and I have made many friends of different cultural backgrounds – Congolese, Zimbabwean, Nigerian, Chinese, Xhosa, Coloured and Indian. Sharing the same spiritual beliefs makes it easier to overcome any cultural differences.*

*And yet I wouldn't be honest if I said I didn't struggle with racial reconciliation. There are things that I still find difficult. Although my natural inclination is to try to understand where somebody else is coming from, at times that willingness to empathize is tested. A case in point would be the "Fees Must Fall" student uprising in 2016. I supported the move to remove the inherent racial bias in tertiary education, but I couldn't grasp how making university free was going to help anyone. Then, when I read about a Wits student wearing a T-shirt that said, "F*ck whites!" I was appalled. How do you engage in constructive dialogue when somebody makes a statement like that?*

I think like many White people, I'm held back by fear. Fear that I don't have a right to speak because of the sins of my people. Fear that our land and possessions will be taken away to right the wrongs of history. Every time Julius Malema[17] speaks about revolution and nationalizing mines and banks, I wonder if we're really heading in that direction. Like Zimbabwe's violent farm invasions or Hugo Chávez's disastrous socialist policies which bankrupted Venezuela.

These fears are real, but they are not insurmountable. I don't think White people should exclude themselves from the national debate on racial reconciliation. At a restitution workshop my husband recently attended, a young Afrikaans man complained that he doesn't feel he has a place any more at the table in South Africa. A Black man responded, "You do, but it's no longer at the head." With grace and humility, we need to have these honest conversations that will help us to see the world a little differently and rebuild the broken walls – one brick at a time.

Katherine is very honest about her fears, yet very hopeful. She reminds me that reconciliation requires everyone to honestly look within, and express both their fears and their hope.

---

17 Leader of the South African political party Economic Freedom Fighters.

Reconciliation at the Grassroots

Ana Luiza De Faria-Lopes Moore is my first White South African friend, and twenty-five years later our friendship is still going strong. We met at Wits University when she opened her heart and family to me. We've shared many special experiences since, including spending a Christmas together in Lisbon with Ana's family.

Born to a Portuguese couple living in Mozambique, Ana came to South Africa with her parents, as a child, after Mozambique became independent of Portugal in 1975. She is now married, has three children, and teaches business studies in high school.

> *I feel very South African. Portuguese is my first language, but I've never lived in Portugal. I was raised in South Africa, I completed my schooling here; I feel like I belong here.*
>
> *I only really began thinking about apartheid after high school, post-1991. I was so ignorant about what was going on when younger. I was in an all-White school and apartheid was just the way things were. Once, we were driving and saw an accident. The injured person was Black. A White ambulance came along but didn't help; they had to wait for a Black ambulance. I was horrified. My parents explained that these are the rules, that's how it works.*
>
> *We lived in the Hill suburb and didn't see much violence in our neighborhood. Soweto is only about twelve kilometers from where I lived, but we never, ever went there. You didn't. Growing up, my mom wouldn't let us out alone. Even when I was eighteen and wanted to go out she was reluctant, for she felt the country was not safe. Even now, I tend to be extra vigilant, as the violence statistics are high. Now it's more about economics, not race. There's unhappiness, corruption; people have been waiting for service delivery for twenty-four years, whether it's getting a house or running water.*
>
> *For me, mixing with others is not an issue. I matriculated at an all-white high school and my first year in university is when I was first exposed to some diversity. That's when I met*

Jesmane. We became friends because we had to do a project. We didn't decide to work together, the lecturer just said, "You three, make it happen." We chose to develop a marketing plan for a funeral parlor, a rather gruesome idea, and quickly bonded. I hadn't had a friend of color before.

She told me about her school, and where and how she lived. We met each other's families. We graduated, started working and decided to take a vacation trip to America, starting in L.A. We spent six months planning it. I thought it would test our friendship, but we had an awesome time. Six weeks, six states. We felt liberated and free as we travelled, our relationship flourished in a neutral place, no history of apartheid loomed. The trip itself gave diverse exposure – a Contiki tour on the West coast with internationals and in New York we stayed with one of Jesmane's friends, Olukemi, who is from Trinidad. In D.C., we stayed with a Kenyan friend.

In South Africa today, we need to become colorblind. We have to use everyone who can possibly make a difference, but there is fear that we are not doing so. I'm a school teacher, my students are seventeen-year-olds. Every time we get into a discussion, the BEE[18] codes come up. The White kids say "We weren't even born in 1994, but we're not going to get a job because only the Blacks will." This is inadvertently building White resentment, and Whites are leaving the country. Masses of professionals are leaving; brain drain, they call it.

To me, reconciliation is about not prejudicing someone or making a judgment call before I know them. Relationships need time to nurture and grow. For example, when my children went to school, they naturally made friends with Black children. Their parents became my friends, but at first we were really just acquaintances.

Time and life events create bonds, and that's what is in process in South Africa. We're all in it together and you need time to allow friendships and trust to grow.

---

18 Black Economic Empowerment.

We need to really listen to each other and not make quick judgment calls based on race. There is so much hatred that we still need to get through, and the big racist incidents are paraded on the media in a sensationalistic manner, making it seem that all relations are bad. I feel at a grassroots level much progress has been made, but this gets overlooked as it's not so exciting. For example, with my high school students, when there are issues that need to be tackled, whether they are White or Black, each case is dealt with sensitively and an appropriate intervention is chosen to assist the child. It's never about "this kid is behaving a certain way because of his color." With my students and their parents, different relationships play out differently and there isn't a pattern based on race. This is good, as I have wider perspective and if there is a relationship with a Black person where the connection is not great, I will not immediately attribute it to our differences in race.

I feel that my role in reconciliation is to continue on this path of education. To offer the same treatment, care and guidance to all children, of all races, is my healing process, my giving back to South Africa. Treating people fairly and with dignity, and looking to the person rather than their race.

Ana is optimistic about moving reconciliation along at a grassroots level, and has seen much success. This spurs me to celebrate the many little steps forward that are rarely noticed, for they too are important.

Intra-Racial Reconciliation

My friend Kanika Dewan offers a different look at reconciliation. Although she and "hers" have been the subject of slights, she was brought up as a global citizen, and has approached her environment in a fluid manner. Her reconciliation has been layered; she never felt strongly at odds with another group and has never felt the need to reconcile with others. However, her struggle with discrimination offers tremendous insight into the need for intra-racial reconciliation.

I was born in Calcutta, India. When I was a few months old, my family moved to Bahrain in the Persian Gulf for business reasons. I've dealt with all kinds of racism, including an almost-violent encounter with anti-immigrant punks on the London subway as a child. But what has really concerned me is intra-group racism.

When I was thirteen I began attending Cheltenham Ladies' College in England, an elite boarding school for girls in Gloucestershire. At first, I gravitated toward the few fellow Indians among the student population. Attaching myself to those who belong to my culture as a way of dealing with my homesickness was strange, given that I had rarely had Indian friends when studying in the British system back in Bahrain. I never really felt a necessity to gravitate towards other Indians. Before my 13th birthday, I just assumed people were people whether Indian or not. I based my friendships on a comfort level versus anyone's ethnic background.

Yet, from the first day at Cheltenham, I sought out other Indians at the school. Initially, the three Indians in my boarding house took me under their wing. They shared memories of Indian food, and liked listening to the Bollywood music cassettes I had brought along. Very soon, however, the two Indian girls whom I felt closest to stopped talking to me. It was as if they didn't want to own their Indianness anymore. They felt that by forming this group they had isolated themselves. While they craved everything Indian in secret, amongst the others they didn't want to acknowledge it. When I was made fun of for using Ayurvedic Indian face creams, they never supported me; when I was bullied, they joined in the laughter to be part of the crew. One of the British girls in the school liked to pull the chair out from under me as I was about to sit down. And she always criticized me, saying "In England we do it this way" and "In England we have that."

I turned to the familiar to gain comfort on school breaks. I hung out with my Indian cousins in England, visited Indian temples, ate Indian food and watched Indian movies. I ended up with a pit in my stomach every time these breaks ended.

Time between our breaks was long and we did not have the solace of frequent phone calls home, so I began to adapt. I returned to what I had been back at home; accepting people for who they are and not where they are from. I began to flourish with friends who weren't Indians. I found that others were intrigued by my Indian culture, and also interested in learning more about the Middle East. To me, this meant there was something exotic and fascinating about being global. I won more friends as I brought them army food packs from the Gulf War; I was their eyes into a world that they had never been part of but was constantly on the news, constantly talked about in our Geography and History classes.

I experienced racism while attending university and graduate school in the U.S. – but it came from other Indians. For example, at The Wharton School of the University of Pennsylvania, the Indians put each other into various categories. They might say other Indians were "ABCD," which stands for "American Born, Confused Desi" and meant Indians born in the U.S. who would not associate with Indians from anywhere else. There were also the "Fresh-Off-the-Boat Indians," who were said to have arrived with suitcases stuffed with food from India and who smelled of curry. These were terms that Indians themselves used to segregate themselves into cliques; a sort of hierarchy of which Indians are cooler and more integrated into the American culture than others.

In the U.S., people often mistook me as being Arab or Latin American. Even other Indians sometimes had trouble identifying me, saying "You're too fair to be Indian," and "Are you sure you are Indian?" My identification with India was complicated. I loved the country where I was born, but thought that not being easy to identify gave me an exclusive status by other Indians – I preferred being seen as an "international Indian." This wasn't really a category, more of a non-category that kept me from being pigeon-holed as ABCD, Fresh-Off-The-Boat or something else, and being treated accordingly. The interesting thing was non-Indians embraced me because they thought I was amorphous; I belonged to everyone because I was an Indian-born, British-educated, American student. I was even accepted by all the Indian groups. I had found the interdependence I was looking for by embracing a borderless self, and enjoyed interactions based on humanity during my best years at University.

I didn't experience any racism when I moved into the world of investment banking at Citigroup. In 2001, I started my own business, Natural Stone Depot, which later transformed into Ka Design Atelier, a vertically integrated, design and build firm which focuses on sustainable life improvement and uses natural materials. Our staff is diverse and discrimination is not a problem – except from Indian companies. When an Indian client hires me, they also hire a White person. This White will be paid more for the design fee, despite my company having won major internationally recognized awards, including placement in the Guinness Book of World Records. When I question this, the Indians say, "You are Indian," as if this somehow explains what lies at the heart of the situation.

Even though I have not experienced tremendous bias about being an Indian – except from some other Indians – after graduation I grew more comfortable with people from my own cultural background. Although I did not grow up in India, when I left the cocoon of the university and began professional life in New York, I found myself moving back toward that cultural group. Maybe you could call this a "mini-reconciliation" with my own group. I spent more time with family and cousins who were in New York, I would take my non-Indian friends to see Bollywood movies, and so on. This was partially driven by my exposure to American values, which preferred independence over interdependence. It made me appreciate the value system I had learned from my parents, the system taken from India. But even though I was identifying more as an Indian, I expanded my circle of friends, embracing anyone who shared my value system, no matter what their background.

I've never really had to reconcile with any other group.

Even in Bahrain where some felt that an Indian can never be a true Bahraini, the bias is very subliminal, and never rose to the point where I felt separated and in need of reconciliation. I remember there were places like the British Beach or British Club, where Indians weren't allowed, but you didn't dwell on this as a child, you accepted it. Also, compared to the rest of the Middle East, Bahrain is a more inviting culture.

What has disturbed me most is the intra-group racism I experienced from Indians. I understand that some of what I experienced can be explained as young girls jockeying to find their place in a boarding school, and immigrants struggling to define themselves within a new culture. Some of it may have been due to the human foibles we all wrestle with. I know that a while ago I had a project in India and many of the workers were lackadaisical and often coming to work drunk. I admit I found myself thinking <u>all</u> Indians must be like this. I was thinking in a racially biased manner toward my own culture! This made me wonder how many times I've done this, and how often I don't live up to my own standards.

Having experienced this, I want to continually remind myself that I have always thought of the world as borderless and our souls as global nationals; everyone is part of the same "energy," and at the same time everyone is a unique human being.

Kanika's story makes it clear that intra-racism can be as hurtful as racism between groups, and there must be an awareness and correction.

My Life Purpose is Reconciliation

Born in a land enmeshed in conflict, my friend Patrick Youssef has dedicated his life to healing and reconciliation. After earning advanced degrees in diplomacy and international law he volunteered for a number of years with the Lebanese Red Cross, hoping that the act of assisting others would help him heal from the trauma of having been raised in a war-torn country. He is currently Deputy Regional Director for Africa for the International Committee of the Red Cross.

Patrick was brought up in the Christian section of Beirut, Lebanon, a city and nation that had been at war with itself and others for decades. Muslims and Christians contested for control of the nation's power structure, even as they struggled to deal with intra-group strife, issues arising from their large Palestinian refugee population, and invasions from Israel and Syria.

I was raised in a community which believed that the adversary is anyone not from our group. That the "others" have betrayed the cause and are aligned with the enemy. That the enemy is the eternal enemy, so any thought of reconciliation is treason.

Fortunately, my family was not driven by hatred. Instead, my parents taught me that this fighting was only for a season; things would get better. They also exposed me to Nelson Mandela and other such models, admonishing me to educate myself rather than to reflexively reach for weapons. Although we are Christians, my parents never said that Islam was bad. They showed me what it was and encouraged me to read the Koran to learn how others believed. They taught me that you cannot succeed until you understand the other side. I read the Koran. And my work has taken me to many Middle Eastern countries and other parts of the world, where I have met with government officials, ethnic and religious leaders, opposition leaders, and regular people.

I learned that whatever their background and religious affiliation, most people are not politicians pushing a cause. Instead, they are just like me, they share my values: raising a family, building their community, searching for peace and prosperity, having some fun.

I come from the Middle East, which is felt to be the source of endless, unsolvable problems. The world feels that this is because of hatred and divisions like the Sunni-Shiite divide. I spent almost ten years working in several countries in the Middle East, meeting people and discovering that no matter what side of which divide they may be on, they are not what you think they would be like from watching television, which is filled with negative images, and they are not the incarnation of their politicians. They have their own identities, and when you meet with them you feel the closeness, you discover they are a lot like you.

We tend to focus on the extreme portrayals created by the politicians and media, but there is much more underneath that. There is a lot of truth in what the media presents, but there is so much more beneath – and that has to be understood in order to reconcile. If you believe that the Middle East is just a bunch of angry people, you will never figure out a way to reconcile them, you will never find the common denominator. I blame the politicians for falling into the trap of religious and ethnic divide and insanity, and I blame the media for playing up this insanity.

We cannot rely on politicians or the media to bring us together, and we cannot rely on the international community: Remember, people in one country are predisposed to think of people in another country in a certain way largely based on what they see in the media. We have to get to the roots, to the people, who most often share the same values you do.

Top-down solutions such as South Africa's Truth and Reconciliation Commission can be very beneficial, but the people have to decide whether or not they are going to reconcile with each other. It is up to them to join together and reconcile based on common interests. Then, as individuals and as groups, they can regain their notion of what it means to belong to a society, to a nation. They can bravely look at the past to uncover the problems, seek restorative justice, and truly reconcile. Restorative justice is a necessary part of reconciliation. Restorative justice is not about retribution, or harsh punishment. It's about revealing the truth and providing compensation. That compensation may be nothing more than learning where your loved ones who disappeared years ago were killed and buried, and being able to rebury them with love. Those who killed them may only serve three or five years in prison, not their entire lives, but the fact that your loved ones have now been buried properly, and that their killers have paid some price, goes a long way toward restoring justice, as well as your dignity and willingness to sit down with the "other side" and begin to reconcile.

Today Patrick works with Red Cross delegations in North and West Africa to ensure that those affected by wars and violence receive the necessary humanitarian assistance and protection, and that the combatants abide by the rules of war, protect civilians, and allow humanitarian organizations access to the vulnerable communities. Although proud of his work, he dreams of one day going back to Lebanon and helping his country heal.

My work puts me in a very good position to do good, but at some point I want to go back to my country and help people reconcile. I can't do that now, for Lebanon is a complex country, still governed by those who took the country into civil war. The old regimes still governing the country doesn't allow much space to younger people like me. If I do go back now, it would have to be because of a special project that calls for me to be sent there.

I'm very frustrated. I'm bringing solutions to other countries; why can't I do the same for my country? I believe it's my job, and every citizen's job, to advance reconciliation. Everybody can do so, in their own way. They can do so through their art or literature, through a project they work on with the "other side," and in so many other ways – even something as simple as sitting down for an open discussion over coffee. This bottom-up approach is very powerful, it can lead to reconciliation without the need for a government-led mechanism.

All over the Middle East people listen to the morning songs of Fairouz. She has been singing for decades, and you hear her music everywhere you go. The fact that she was born to a Christian Maronite family in Lebanon doesn't matter – people love her music in every country in the Middle East. There are so many things that we all love, so many values we share. We can build on our shared values to reconcile. We must do so, and it is everyone's responsibility to do so.

Patrick inspires me tremendously with his passion for reconciliation, both in his home country, Lebanon, and everywhere in the world.

The Mosaic of Reconciliation

The stories in this chapter touch upon a few of the many paths to reconciliation. From each, I learned something. Clearly, there is no single path to reconciliation; the approaches taken by my friends are all appropriate. Some have completed the journey to reconciliation, some are working on it, and some have concluded that the time is not yet ripe. I believe that we should always aspire to reconciliation, and at the same time recognize that different people are at different stages of their journey, and are trying to reconcile with people and groups who are on journeys of their own. I believe that reconciliation is worth working towards, so I hope the aspiration remains strong.

The one certainty that emerges, however, is the importance of seeking out stories, whether they are from "your side" or the "other side," or perhaps some "side" you never thought of before. There is inspiration everywhere and we never know where the stimulus, the warmth and the healing, will come from.

My mentor, Russell Hawkins, is a Black-American who was raised as a "military brat" and lived and went to school on U.S. Army bases in Germany, Puerto Rico, and the United States. He experienced his share of prejudice growing up, once being called the "N-word" to his face. He has lived and worked in South Africa for over twenty years, and while here encouraged me to study at Harvard, making me believe that it was possible.

Russell believes that "reconciliation requires open, honest, sincere communication between people and seeing people for what they are, not for what they look like. It requires being willing to listen and to learn. It requires being willing to say 'I was wrong.' And it's a process, not a product. Wounds don't heal that easily, particularly wounds that arise out of the horrible, dehumanizing, and sometimes deadly things that people do to each other."

It's true, wounds don't always heal that easily. It's also true that clinging too tightly to the unhappy past can stop us from moving forward. Only forward movement that can take us to a better tomorrow for ourselves, our families, our groups – and yes, even those who have harmed us. But as we have seen, reconciliation can be a very difficult process even for those who genuinely want to make peace with the "others" and create an inclusive, prosperous future for all.

9

FEAR OF LACK & DESIRE TO DOMINATE

I'VE LOOKED AT reconciliation on an individual and societal level; now I'd like to build on this by adding a national and international level. This requires us to broaden our view, to look at issues over a long time scale through the lens of history.

History is an attempt to understand why we as societies and nations have done what we did. There are various theories as to what propels history, including race and racism. Race has certainly been an important driver of events, for we can easily see ourselves in fellow members of our racial group, with whom we share ancestry, skin color, religion, customs, language, and more. This makes race a convenient way to understand and organize ourselves as we compete for resources and the reins of power, attempt to reorder society according to our desires, and otherwise assert dominance.

Race and racism take on even more importance once we identify members of our race as "us" and anyone else as "them," then blame "them" for our problems. "They" are not like us, they wear different clothing, worship in odd ways, talk in strange tongues, and otherwise parade their differences.

We easily magnify the differences between "us" and "them" in our minds, leaping from "they are not like us" to "they are a threat" to "they should be kept out"; from "we are deserving of more" to "they are deserving of less." In extreme cases, as with the Nazis and the Rwandan Hutu, we may leap even further, from "they are not us" to "they are less than human and are a danger to us." When we reach this point we can easily discard qualms about destroying "them," for they are no different than the rats and cockroaches who invade our homes. In fact, exterminating "them" is necessary and positive, for in eradicating them we are cleansing the world. Unfortunately, a great deal of history can be cast in terms such as these.

While there is no doubt that race and racism are important drivers of history, I believe that it's not always solely about race and racism. Indeed, if I were to choose a single primary driving force in history, it would be fear. From well before the time history was recorded, mankind has been filled with the fear of lack – lack of food, land, water, key minerals, and other resources. This fear, in turn, has driven the desire to dominate others so that we may take what we need, and often way more.

Fear and the desire to dominate have been the primary drivers of history as various groups have struggled to ensure their futures, sometimes viciously so. For example, in the late 1100s and early 1200s, Genghis Khan unified the warring nomadic tribes of Mongolia and then conquered foreign lands, rapidly creating an empire encompassing huge swaths of China and central Asia. His descendants then grew the empire further in Asia, Europe and the Middle East. Many centuries later, the Zulu nation was similarly built on the desire for land and power. Shaka Zulu, leader of the Zulu people, combined weapons technology with a brilliant sense of tactics to first defend his tribe against threatening neighbors, then to dominate and consolidate other tribes. Striking out in multiple directions, Shaka Zulu conquered one group after another, rewarding chiefdoms that submitted to his protection while brutally punishing those which would not. By 1819 the Zulu nation had become the largest ever in the southeast of Africa and Shaka Zulu was called the "Black Napoleon."

Fear and the desire to dominate have driven conflicts in Europe and America, as well. For example, the infamous St. Bartholomew's Day massacre of 1572, which saw French Catholics massacre French Protestants, was part of a struggle without a racial underpinning. So was the largely European and Anglo Saxon bloodbath known as World War I, which led to the deaths of over sixteen million soldiers and civilians. The primary belligerents fought over land, power, prestige and other non-racial elements. And the Cold War, which ran from the late 1940s through the fall of the Soviet Union, was driven by economic and political ideology.

Certainly, it is tempting to group by race when hit with fear of lack, whether we find ourselves competing for resources that truly are scarce, or simply felt to be. And struggles for resources and dominance have often been cast in racial terms, including the 19th century American concept of Manifest Destiny and the 20th century South African construct called apartheid, both of which held that a certain group was deserving of all the land and other resources it could lay even the most tenuous claim to, while those already present on the land deserved nothing more than a quick warning before they were swept away or effectively enslaved.

But it is important to remember that race can be a difficult subject to pin down. For one thing, the definition of "race" has changed over time, as have the definitions of "us" and "other." In the United States, for example, those who traced their ancestry back to Mexico were officially classified as White until the 1930s, when they were shifted to the new classification of Hispanic.[19] The South African apartheid regime, not sure how to handle Japanese, Koreans, and certain other East Asians, classified them as "honorary whites." Japanese were granted this designation because of growing trade between Japan and South Africa, which shows how economics can influence racial calculation.

Even when people are acknowledged as belonging to the same race as "us" they may be considered to be more like "them," whoever the most distasteful "them" of the moment may be. When the "Great Hunger" prompted up to two million Irish to immigrate to the United States in the mid-19th century,[20] the new arrivals were viewed with

19 "Race Timeline – Go Deeper." PBS.org, 2003. Accessible at http://www.pbs.org/race/000_About/002_04-background-02-12.htm. Viewed April 24, 2018.

20 Christopher Klein. "When America Despised the Irish: The 19th Century's Refugee Crisis." History.com. March 16, 2017. Accessible at https://www.history.com/news/when-america-despised-the-irish-the-19th-centurys-refugee-crisis. Viewed July 16, 2018.

disdain. Despite the fact that their skin was quite clearly white, they were perceived to be lazy, prone to criminality and disease, lacking in decency, a drain on society and, perhaps worst of all, known to be Catholic rather than Protestant. Thus, they were shunted off to lesser neighborhoods and jobs. It seemed impossible to imagine a time when the Irish would be seen as "us" by white America, yet that is exactly what happened. A similar arc of abhorrence and acceptance encompasses the story of numerous groups in America.

Who Is "Us?"

Race can be a large part of the "us" versus "them" calculation, yet it loses relevance when the fear level drops. When that happens, groups may coalesce around other makers of "us-ness."

In modern times, demographic, social, and economic factors have combined with the ease of long-distance travel to produce many cities where various peoples mix. In these areas, people form communities in multiple ways and the definition of "us" and "them" can take on new meanings not necessarily connected to race. I know that as I mix with people of more races, ethnicities, religions, educational backgrounds, and other identifiers than I can count, I often find my definition of "us" shifting according to the situation and the people involved. Indeed, I don't have an all-encompassing rule to describe who is "us" for me. It changes with the context. In some situations, "us" is people who love to travel, are open to diverse experiences, care about making an impact, and are passionate about nutrition and fitness. On a recent trip to Mongolia with a mixed international group, I shared a ger[21] with Silvia, a bubbly Italian woman living in the United States, and we developed a rapid bond built on our shared world view, love of new and exotic experiences, being in unspoilt nature in a hardly-traversed terrain, experiencing a new culture, and dancing around a bonfire with the group 'till the wee hours. In situations like these, I feel very cosmopolitan. In another context, when I'm meeting with fellow

---

21 A ger is a tent with one door and no windows that nomadic and rural Mongolians live in. It's the same as a Russian yurt.

members of the African Women Chartered Accountants Association, I feel my identity as a Black woman more strongly.

Racism, Fear of Lack, Desire to Dominate Intermingle

When thinking of conflict between individuals, groups, and nations, I imagine a spectrum with racism on one end and the desire to dominate on the other. Some conflicts are driven largely by racism, as were the activities of the American Ku Klux Klan and the Rwandan Hutu's massacre of the Tutsi in the 1990s. At the other end of the spectrum you'll find clashes like the early 16th century brotherly battle for the throne of the sophisticated and extensive Inca Empire. Upon the death of Emperor Huayna Capac and his designated successor, two of the late emperor's sons took up arms against each other in a contest for control. There were no racial issues at stake in this war. Something very similar occurred in the 15th century Wars of the Roses, a struggle between rival factions of the British aristocracy – it was cousin competing against cousin to see who would sit on the throne of England and enjoy the resulting power, land, and prestige.

Most conflicts are somewhere between the two ends of the spectrum, mixing racism with the desire to dominate. In some conflicts the cause was commercial, co-mingled with a racial element. This happened in South Africa, with the first group of Dutch settlers in the mid-1600s being primarily interested in establishing supply stations to service trading ships making the long journey between Europe and Asia to advance the lucrative Dutch spice trade in Asia. Supplementing their spice trade profits, the Dutch East India Company also traded slaves, giving their activities a racial component. Subsequently, in South Africa, the indigenous Khoisan farm laborers were indentured, beginning the process that led to severe racial policies. Between 1881 and 1914, during what was known as the "Scramble for Africa," large swaths of African land were colonized and divided by Europeans who cast greedy eyes on the continent's vast mineral wealth.

The same mixture of racism and desire to dominate led to the infamous "Trail of Tears" in the United States. By 1830, many Native Americans had already been dispossessed and forced to move to distant areas as White settlement spread. But large numbers of Native Americans remained in the southeastern section of the country, often living on choice land that the Whites coveted. During the 1830s, as many as 100,000 Native Americans were rounded up at bayonet point – thousands at a time – and forced to walk from their ancestral lands in Florida, Georgia, North Carolina, Tennessee and Alabama all the way to modern-day Oklahoma, where land had been set aside for them. The conditions of the forced journey were shameful and beyond cruel; not enough food and other supplies were provided, and disease was rampant. Some 15,000 of the 100,000 who were forced to march died on the journey, earning the series of removals the nickname "The Trail of Tears."[22]

Unfortunately, conflict between groups continues. Today, the battle in South Sudan between the Dinka and the Nuer, the nation's two largest ethnic groups, is nuanced and driven by a mix of racism, competition for resources – namely oil – the desire to control, poor governance, political allegiances, and external factors.

No matter where a conflict falls on the spectrum, however, fear is often the underlying issue. With the most extreme examples of racism, the fear is about the horrible damage that the "other" does simply by existing. With the most extreme examples of desire to dominate, the fear is purely of lack. It may be expressed in terms of gain, as in, "If we built a place to service our trading ships we could make more money," but underneath even the most obsessive drive for gain tends to be the fear of lack.

So when considering conflicts between groups where race is often cited as the sole factor, we would do well to remember that underlying conflict is fear. Race may be the obvious and immediate cause, but it is most often underpinned by fear of lack and the desire to dominate. While it's true that reducing racism can assuage some fear, it is equally important to attack the fear directly. When fear of lack has been removed from the equation, the importance of race plummets.

---

22 Elizabeth Prine Pauls. "Trail of Tears." *Encyclopedia Britannica*. Revised, 2008. Accessible at https://www.britannica.com/event/Trail-of-Tears. Viewed July 31, 2018.

Professor Robert Livingston of Harvard University points out that humans have a propensity to form non-inclusive groups and hierarchies. While this may be inborn and immutable, we need not decide who is "us" and "them" strictly on the basis of race. That is largely a subconscious choice that can be, and often is, overridden by other issues.

The question is, how can we ensure that people forego the easy choice to understand issues solely on the basis of race, and instead approach them with an eye to overcoming fear so that we may all advance together?

Our Choices to Make

The fear that drives conflict will likely grow as competition for resources intensifies. The worldwide population will increase from about 7.6 billion in 2018 to nearly 10 billion by 2050. Demand for food and water will rise, placing severe strains on the ability of many nations to provide for their people. Add the challenges posed by climate change, and you can imagine wars being threatened, or actually breaking out, over food and water, to say nothing of the many other resources we desire.

Certain nations may respond to this by bulking up their military, economic, and technological might, preparing to take what they need to survive. This could be a very effective approach for some countries, yet would likely lead to widespread deprivation, to say nothing of the damage caused by any wars that may result. With today's sophisticated nuclear and cyber weaponry, that damage could be catastrophic. And, of course, most nations are not strong enough to even contemplate such an approach.

Given this very serious threat, it is imperative that we stop competing with each other on the basis of "what's good for my group," regardless of how "us" is defined. Instead, we should be thinking in terms of creating the best possible future for all people and peoples. And that requires reframing and making choices; clear, distinct choices about how we see ourselves in relation to other people, and how we understand our obligations to each other. It means choosing to do things now, even small things that can make the future better for everyone.

In my own life, I learned that it is possible to take small steps forward in the face of overwhelming odds and opposition. I learned, for example, that it was possible for a downtrodden girl to strive for education despite the obstacles of apartheid, and that this was possible thanks to the unwavering support of her parents and other family members, as well as her faith in herself, in the future, and in God. I learned the power of delayed gratification, and that discipline and diligence with studies would pay off in the long run. I learned to identify and fill in the gaps in my education and life that had been caused by my township upbringing.

I truly believe we can begin taking small steps now and calling on whatever inspires one individually to ensure a better future for everyone. Although we can never be sure exactly how the future will play out, we can, as individuals, societies and nations, act on the assumption that positive perspectives developed and choices made today will result in beneficial results later.

To that end, we can make a number of personal choices. We can choose to recognize that fear underlies most conflict between individuals and groups, and we can choose to fight fear by focusing our energies on ensuring that everyone's needs will be met, now and in the future.

We can choose to see ourselves as belonging first and foremost to the "us" of humanity. This reduces the fear that "my" group will be harmed by "yours," for we all are part of the same "us."

We can choose to be part of diverse groups, rather than remaining solely within our own group or community. Joining groups where the "us" is defined in various ways, and in different ways from group to group, reminds us that race is not always the defining factor.

We can choose to redefine our view of the future so that no matter what the present circumstances, no matter what the actual or perceived lacks we face as individuals and groups, we believe that it *is* possible to create a prosperous and inclusive tomorrow for everyone.

We can also make choices as societies and nations. We can choose to level the playing field so that everyone, regardless of race, gender, and other factors has the opportunity to rise as far as their talents and energy will take them. This has the added benefit of increasing diversity, for more members of previously ignored groups will be able to contribute their energy and ideas.

We can choose to make education a priority, so our youth are prepared for an increasingly technological future.

We can choose to support the use and development of technologies that will spread empowerment to all, especially the hundreds of millions of poor and disempowered people who rarely look to the future with hope, for their hopes have rarely been rewarded in the past.

We can choose to promote diversity, for when people of different backgrounds are brought together, in the workplace and the coffee shop, in schools and in playgrounds, they learn to trust and respect each other. When they are brought together in offices, laboratories, theatres, and other places of work, creation, and inspiration, the resulting mixture of ideas can create a wonderful new mosaic filled with new ideas and inventions.

In the Appendix, I take a closer look at technology and diversity. Meanwhile, it's time to consider the effects of reframing. That is, of learning to reinterpret what has happened in a new light, so that we may respond to it in a more positive and inclusive way.

We'll look at reframing on a personal and group level, and see how we can reframe the past and future as much as we can the present. Indeed, we must reframe the past in order to reinterpret the present, and doing both makes it possible to envision and truly believe in a future where everyone's needs are met.

REFRAMING TO REDISCOVER HOPE

WE ARE ALL authors, crafting the story of our lives. We continually write and rewrite, interpret and reinterpret what has happened to and around and because of us, reshaping the narrative in an attempt to make sense of it all. An understanding that worked at one point in our lives fails us at another point, and we struggle to compose a different interpretation – to reframe what has happened so that we may understand it in a new light.

Some of us create stories in which we are the heroic protagonist, others, stories in which we are the weary victim. Some cling fast to a few major themes, insisting that each new piece of information be made to conform with the existing interpretation, while others are open to new understandings that may arise as new information challenges old ideas. No matter how we choose to craft our story, it is much more than a personal history. It is our understanding of ourselves, our origins, and potential. As such, it goes a long way toward determining our future.

As our story is constantly being extended and revised, our interpretations of ourselves and the world are reinforced, changed, or both – we cannot escape that fact. What we can do is to take our mental pen in hand and become the conscious, deliberate authors of our story. We can choose to better understand, and sometimes reinterpret our past, and in so doing, begin to change what will be written tomorrow.

Joy in Crafting My New Script

For communities which have been repressed, as well as for individuals, reframing the past can make the future seem much more hopeful and promising. I have seen how reframing the past has gone a long way to soothing my pain while simultaneously making me more resilient, appreciative of all those who have loved and aided me, and fueling me with hope.

For example, I reframed my understanding of my father as I learned more about his past. He was no longer the weakling who had failed his family. Instead, he was resilient and courageous, a loving husband and father who continued to put one foot in front of the other in the face of apartheid. All he wanted to do was to keep working to support us, even after his exhausting and exploitative work contract that triggered a nervous breakdown – and even though his illness forced him to surrender the pride that came with being a skilled construction carpenter and toil instead as a laborer. Developing this new understanding of my father's story gave me a sense of care towards blue-collar workers who can so easily be treated unjustly. Today, in various company meetings and board rooms I am involved in, I speak out against exploitation of lower-level employees who can't defend themselves. Reframing my view of my father required talking to him and filling in missing information about his life and struggle, and I am sorry that it look so long for me to do so.

Reinterpreting my poor upbringing was not a simple matter of filling in the missing facts, for I knew too well how poor we had been. I remembered clearly the taunts of schoolmates mocking my shabby clothing and battered school case, and I could easily see, in my mind's eye, my mother returning from a long day's work and commute, moody and snappy, feeling the weight of the world on her shoulders as she struggled to be the main provider for our family. Unfortunately, I had allowed these negatives to push aside all the many wonderful aspects of my childhood, including a loving and supportive family, the magnificent wall Grampa built for us, being raised with a twin sister who doubled as a study buddy, and the love and prayers that flowed so freely from my blind grandmother. I had allowed my unhappy memories to overwhelm this and so much more, including the many hours Uncle Reg spent with my sister and me, tutoring us in mathematics so that we might have a chance of rising above what seemed to be our limited futures.

I have reframed the story of my past to emphasize a truth I had overlooked: my family gave me the essential things I needed to succeed, personally and professionally. Reframing my childhood in this manner gave me fortitude, and filled me with gratitude. It helped me recognize the source of my passion for uplifting poor people, with a special affinity for those in emerging markets. I recently reframed large sections of my story after visiting the Slave Lodge, a museum of the history of slavery in South Africa, located in Cape Town. My purpose in visiting was to conduct research for this book, and to understand the truth of the origins of the Coloured community,[23] which has largely been erased from history. The trip was successful in that I gleaned the necessary facts, but gained so much more.

Initially, I felt disheartened and lame as I learned of the horrendous cruelty my slave ancestors faced. I felt shame and, for a few days, was overwhelmed by the helplessness of their situation. After the horror had passed, I struggled to re-frame the experience from a festering wound that holds me back to a positive narrative of fortitude and hope that takes me forward. Reframing was difficult, for I felt stuck in the pain and trauma of my slave ancestors. It was only after I deliberately worked on reframing the story of my slave ancestors, and worked through a few iterations that gave positive interpretations, that I became unstuck.

My reframing includes a better understanding of who these people were. I had seen them as victims of the slaver's net to be pitied. Instead, at the Slave Lodge I learned that many of the slaves were snatched from far-away lands that in the past boasted marvelous kingdoms

---

23 The story of the Coloured people in South Africa reaches back to 1658, with the arrival of the first slave ships at the Cape of Good Hope. The first coloured children were born soon thereafter, giving the Coloured people a history of about three hundred and sixty years. Half of this time, one hundred and eighty years, was spent in slavery, with a vast portion of the remaining half spent in oppressive conditions akin to slavery. (While slavery was abolished in the Cape in 1834, slaves were indentured to their former owners up to 1838.)

and cultures – including India and Indonesia, which are today among the G20 countries. So I most emphatically am not the child of the victims of the world. Instead, I am the daughter of the Khoisan people of the Kalahari Desert, whose unique click languages are felt to be among the very first developed by humans. I am a daughter of Tamil Nadu, the Indian state whose official language, Tamil, is one of the oldest languages in the world and a classical language of India. I am the daughter of Sri Lanka, of Java, Bali, and Sulawesi in Indonesia, Madagascar, Mozambique, all ancient peoples and cultures I can point to with pride.

I am the daughter of smart, creative, and proud people who happened to have been impressed into slavery, yet who clung to their pride and hope in the future, who contributed significantly to the Afrikaans language and South African culture. They have produced outstanding individuals across all spheres such as sprinter Wayde van Niekerk, winner of Olympic gold; acclaimed rapper AKA; social entrepreneur Marlon Parker; tech entrepreneur Stafford Masie, the former CEO of Google South Africa; and businesswoman Cathy Smith, MD of SAP Africa. The Coloured community was the source and inspiration for the musical play *Kat and the Kings*, with music by the late Taliep Petersen, which showcases the Coloured culture of Cape Town's District 6 in the 1950s, before the Coloureds were forcibly evicted and the area made "Whites Only." *Kat and the Kings* has played on both Broadway and London's West End theatrical district, receiving top American and British awards. And as I write this, *Nommer 37*, a movie set in the Cape Flats, a Coloured poor area, is being shown in New York and Los Angeles.

The fact that a sprinkling of Coloured people are rising to new and previously impossible heights does not erase the many social ills plaguing the Coloured community, including drugs, alcohol, gangsterism and unemployment. Still, refashioning my story in this positive manner has given me a sense of pride for what the slave community has contributed to my make-up and culture. It has also connected me to, and given me a glimpse into the Black-American slave experience.

Reframing just these three threads of my story – my father, our family poverty, and the South African slave experience – has made a tremendous difference in my life. Collectively, they have re-channeled the pain, anger, fear, unfairness, and frustration that the past had written into my future, so determinedly and for so long, and given me a new script filled with hope, pride and strength.

Reframing for Individuals and Groups

There is no doubt that we constantly write and rewrite, interpret and reinterpret the stories of our lives, and that what is written in the past and present chapters has a large influence over what will be written on future pages. As far as I'm concerned, the only issue is whether or not we choose to consciously guide the process, to decide who will be the author/interpreter of our life story, and in so doing, to open ourselves up to all the possibilities that are within our reach.

Scholars have written about the process of reframing in much more detail than I have space for here. Bill George, co-author of *Discover Your True North*, has useful suggestions for going back into the crucible of your life story, turning wounds into pearls and, in so doing, finding places of passion linked to your calling.

Some people have asked me if reframing is of any value to those who struggle with globalization, automation, and other world-wide changes that have cost many people their jobs and positions in society. They have asked me how, for example, American factory workers who have lost their well-paying jobs and who feel threatened by globalization and changing demographics can reframe their life stories when their futures seem so grim. My answer is, their unhappy outlook is exactly the reason they should reinterpret their stories. Reframing will not magically cause a factory to open down the road and offer them jobs. It can, however, allow them to tap into the strength and determination their ancestors displayed as they endured the Great Depression; the courage and sense of sacrifice as they crossed oceans and continents to defeat their opponents during World War II; the pride and joy of moving into the middle class and buying their first homes, and more. Reframing can reconnect them with the optimism they once felt, optimism since obscured by fear and doubt. Their fears and doubts are very real – but so are the love and hope they once basked in. Embracing fear and doubt is tempting, but it closes one down rather than opening one up to new possibilities.

I believe that this approach to reframing can be helpful to everyone and every group. For all, the ideas are the same – only the sources of love and strength and inspiration are different.

Reframing is not about getting back at someone or something you feel has harmed you, nor is it limited to striving for something you want. It is about discovering the forgotten courage and optimism, the hope and love and joy that lies somewhere in your past, and infusing your future with the same. And when the infusion has taken place, you see the world through a new lens. You are better prepared to take advantage of opportunities that open up, or to create new opportunities of your own. That is the promise of reframing.

And there's an additional possibility. When enough of us have reframed our life stories in a positive manner; when enough of us have written our futures full of hope, optimism, and possibilities, we will see many of our social and economic woes remedied. It's inevitable, for when people see bountiful possibilities for themselves, they need not worry if others gain as well. In fact, we may all realize that in helping others, we help ourselves.

11

STORIES & INSPIRATIONAL LEADERSHIP

I TRULY BELIEVE in the power of reframing and other approaches to healing ourselves, our communities, and our nations that I've touched upon in this book. I hope that people across the globe will find them to be helpful. Most of all, I hope that we keep sharing our stories.[24]

I've told you much of my story in this book. I hope it has touched you, whether you suffered because of racial or other forms of bigotry, stood on the sidelines and watched such things happen, or found yourself in the position of harming others. While working on this book, I spoke to many people and heard many stories that made me teary-eyed for their pain, yet they also left me inspired, for I saw how many of them had risen above the past and extended their hands across the gulf to others. I hope that you, too, will share your story with the "others" in your life and will listen to their stories with an open heart. I hope that as you share your stories, you will speak of your feelings on identity, choice, forgiveness and lingering emotions, re-framing, views of the "other" and on reconciliation, and everything else that you have deliberately kept bottled up or have not realized is

---

24 For more on telling stories, see the "Public Narrative Participant Guide," which is adapted from the works of Harvard University Professor Marshall Gantz, accessible at https://www.ndi.org/sites/default/files/Public%20Narrative%20Participant%20Guide.pdf. For more on inspirational leadership, see Dean Williams's book Real Leadership: Helping People and Organizations Face Their Toughest Challenges. Berrett-Koehler Publishers, 2005.

bottled up within you. I hope that you will begin by making time for self-compassion and reflecting on your feelings and views, for sadly, most of us hurry on with life without stopping to consider whether we need to devote some time and effort to healing. I also hope that once you have had the time to reflect, you speak with honesty to and compassion for your listener, for every conversation is an opportunity to bridge for authentic connection.

Sharing our stories is important, for as they are told, we move from being the faceless "them" to taking on individual identities. Some people are indeed stuck firmly in their prejudice, but I have found that many are willing to meet you part way, if only you will listen to them, hear their stories, and acknowledge their vulnerability, pain, anger, resentment, fear, or anything else. I have found that when we listen, we can find the common threads and expressions of humanity in our stories; we can find the common wounds and attempts to heal from being victims and perpetrators of racism. Most of us feel horrified and helpless when violent racist acts are paraded across the media, for despite our human flaws and personal errors, we imagine and hope for a world that is truly non-racist. We yearn for leaders who will take us to this better world, not realizing that we can all be those leaders. And when we become those leaders, we are like mothers birthing new life into our families, circles of friends, workplaces, communities, nations, and ourselves.

The world is divided and fractured more than ever now, it is crippled by fear of lack and of the other. It seems that we are going backwards. That's why now is the time for us to share our stories and to become inspirational leaders. The time is now because ethnic, racial, and other forms of bigotry and hatred continue to fester globally and new contentions are arising as migrants make their way into various countries. Lingering bigotry and hatred are like a cancer that has not been completely purged from the system, and as long as a single cell remains – even if in remission – the body cannot be completely whole. It only takes one potentially unjustified killing of a Black civilian by a White police officer, one violent rampage against an immigrant, an attack on a place of worship, or any other such incident, to cause the cancer to begin replicating itself and spread far and wide. It must stop now, and we can stop it.

That is why now is the time for each of us to become inspirational leaders. Now is the time for us to bridge for authentic connections, even if we must sometimes do so through our own pain, and must override old patterns of default reactions.

Now is the time for businesses to embrace diversity by creating enabling environments for diversity in staff and the supply chain, investing financial and human capital in entrepreneurs from oppressed groups, and developing tech-enabled innovative solutions (including market-based solutions) to the socioeconomic problems affecting oppressed groups.

Now is the time for the media to use its public platform to encourage unity and understanding amongst different race groups and to discourage generalizations and racial stereotyping.

Now is the time for all racial groups to deal with issues that may be holding them back from reconciliation. For those who come from groups that have oppressed others, this includes dealing with any feelings of superiority – even if subliminal – and caring about and playing a role in addressing the economic inequality that impacts current or formerly oppressed groups. For those who have been oppressed, this includes addressing residual resentment and unforgiveness.

Now is the time for the government to provide moral and inspirational leadership that unifies while quelling racism, to celebrate both national identity and individual ethnicities. It is also time to intentionally deal with the inequality that tends to go hand in hand with racism and discrimination. Notwithstanding Singapore's authoritarian government and widening income gap, it is notable for a successful dual strategy that achieved both national integration and pluralism in relation to its multi-ethnic population, categorized as Chinese, Malays, Indians, and Others.

Now is the time for inspirational leaders to move the needle and change the hearts of individuals and nations by bringing people together. The Rev. Martin Luther King was one such inspirational leader; he knew how to invite everyone to join the united "we," as he did when he reminded us that "When we allow freedom to ring . . . we will be able to speed up the day when all of God's children, black men and white men, Jews and Gentiles, Protestants and Catholics, will be able to join hands and sing in the words of that old Negro spiritual, 'Free at last, Free at last, Great God a-mighty, We are free at last.'"

Who is today's Rev. King? Who is our Nelson Mandela, our Abraham Lincoln? Who will inspire us to rise above color, gender, wealth, and all the other barriers to turn a bunch of "thems" into a united "we"? Who will simultaneously praise our uniqueness while reminding us that we are all a part of the larger community and that we are ultimately all one?

I cannot say who the leaders history remembers and writes of will be, but I can say with absolute certainty that everyone can inspire others with their forgiveness, kindness, and authentic desire to connect. Each and every one of us can be an inspirational leader amongst our families and friends, and in the workplace and place of worship. Each and every one of us can be a "mini King," and from this many, a few will rise to inspire us to even greater heights.

Of this I am sure.

Appendix:
Tech-Enabled Impact Investing & Diversity

TECHNOLOGY IS A powerful tool for relieving conflict, for it can reduce the fear of lack. Indeed, it can even extend certain resources, turning lack into plenty. When, for example, we can desalinate massive quantities of water for pennies per gallon, and provide inexpensive ways for hundreds of millions of subsistence and small-scale farmers to raise enough crops for their families, with extra to sell, the age-old fears of lack of water and food are calmed. When we can provide inexpensive, portable and easy-to-use diagnostic tests to millions of people, we reduce pressure on the health-care system and the fear of lack of care. When we develop rural communities and give rural people access via their phones to health, education and agriculture resources, we can reduce the fear of excessive and uncontrollable migration to cities.

My friend John Harthorne founded and heads up the world's largest startup accelerator. Headquartered in Boston, *MassChallenge* supports innovators and entrepreneurs who utilize technology to tackle issues related to poverty and other seemingly intractable problems affecting the First World and emerging markets, including agriculture, health, water, racial reconciliation, and flow of donor funding. Among the many socially minded start-ups encouraged by MassChallenge are:

• *Kheyti,* a non-profit which has developed a low-cost modular greenhouse kit bundled with education and services. Kheyti's goal is to help subsistence farmers who struggle to produce enough food to feed their families in the face of climate change, difficulty affording quality seeds, personal illness, and any number of other situations which can eat up an entire year's effort. With their crops protected in a low-cost greenhouse that reduces water usage by up to 90 percent, people can farm under adverse conditions yet grow seven times more food. With enough food to feed their families and surplus to sell, they can escape the annual struggle to survive and begin to accumulate financial reserves. Kheyti is currently building its proof of concept with 300 farmers in India.

•	*Diagnostics for All,* a non-profit which has created a paper-based medical test designed for the 60 percent of the developing world that lives beyond the reach of urban hospitals and medical infrastructure. The test requires just a single drop of blood to diagnose several conditions, all on the same paper-like "test sheet." It's as simple as putting a tiny bit of your blood on different areas of the sheet and reading the results. The test is quick, inexpensive, and portable, which makes it invaluable for people who don't usually have access to health care, as well as those who cannot afford such care even if they have access. Diagnostics for All's tests are currently being used in Kenya and other parts of sub-Saharan Africa, as well as Vietnam.

•	*Resolute Marine Energy,* a for-profit which utilizes "unique technology that harnesses ocean wave energy to produce fresh water in areas where large-scale seawater desalination plants are too expensive and take too long to build." It is currently being employed in the United States and in Cape Town, South Africa, which is suffering from a severe water shortage.

•	*OtheReality,* a non-profit founded by a sixteen-year-old high school student which uses virtual reality to help you see life through the eyes of the "other." Experiencing the lives of people on the other side of the divide promotes empathy and reconciliation between men and women, Blacks and Whites, Israelis and Palestinians, and other groups at odds with each other. The company hopes "that OtheReality will be part of Schools' curricula all-around the globe, promoting positive social change and cultural understanding, while using technology to fight against prejudice and intolerance." The company is working to launch a pilot program in Israel.

•	*Aid:Tech,* a for-profit which uses blockchain technology to increase transparency, servicing NGOs, governments, and corporates. Thanks to the blockchain technology, everyone can clearly see and track how an organization's money is being disbursed. This means there is less likely to be "leakage," so trust improves and everyone is more confident that their donations will be used appropriately. Aid:Tech's software is currently being used to help provide aid to homeless women in Ireland, handle social welfare payments in Jordan, and facilitate the transfer of remittances to Serbia.

There are many other ways in which technology can be used to help refugees, the unemployed, poor farmers, those who are sick but do not have access to doctors, and others struggling with seemingly intractable issues. Sometimes the solutions only require that existing technology be deployed in novel ways. Other times, the problems require new or hybrid technology, such as a combination solar energy generator and water desalinator, built into a little shed, that is efficient enough to satisfy the needs of a large village, robust enough to last for two decades, and profitable enough to pay for itself within a few years of operation – all at fairly low initial cost. With the electricity generated by the solar panel, villagers can charge their phones and even if they only own a basic feature phone, can then have access to health, educational, agricultural, and other forms of technology. They can create internet-based microbusinesses that offer them brand-new ways of generating income and building wealth. As individual income levels rise, the entire village can avail itself of better nutrition and health-care services. They can embark on projects to improve neighborhood safety and hygiene, and otherwise lift themselves out of what may have been generations of poverty and severely limited horizons.

Thanks to John Harthorne's MassChallenge, and others like it, money and resources are being channeled to start-ups working to help people at the base of the pyramid, bringing electricity and clean water to underserved areas, desalinating large amounts of ocean water, and otherwise helping to heal and improve the world. MassChallenge is a great start. Think how much more could be done if we could get more funding to, and create an enabling environment for, the people who are literally trying to change the world.

Tech Can Bring the City to the Countryside

Part of changing the world is helping the hundreds of millions of unbanked people to receive and send money across national lines, quickly, easily, and inexpensively. Transferring money from one country to another has long been a problem for migrant workers, including the several hundred thousand Filipinos and Indonesians in Hong Kong, who are mainly women working as domestic helpers. These migrant workers, who are often the main source of support for their families back home, typically work six days a week and spend their one day off per week standing in hours-long lines at money shops – and, of course, paying a fee to send money home.

My friend Max Liu founded EMQ, a financial settlement network that provides the infrastructure to make financial services more accessible to the millions of people across Asia who do not have access to banks. Partnering with banks, and working with regulators to ensure that his firm toes the legal line, EMQ provides the underlying technology used by the Chinese Internet giant Tencent to support its We Remit application across the Philippines and Indonesia, allowing migrant workers to transfer funds to their home countries via their phones, instantly, at any time, at a fraction of the previous cost. Their families can pick up the money at a convenient cash point.

Creating this system required developing software that was intuitive and easy to use. Deploying such software has had the "side effect" of drawing more and more people onto the internet, via their phones, where they can access not only EMQ, but numerous other applications created to address general and maternal health, sanitation, insect control, and crop protection, which are among the many issues that rural people routinely struggle with. Until recently, despite outreach efforts, the best bet for rural people was to move to the cities. Unfortunately, they often lacked the education, skills, and connections to succeed in urban areas, were frequently resented by those already there, and strained city infrastructure to the breaking point.

Rather than being forced to trek to the unwelcoming city, the city can now come to them, so to speak. In addition to greatly improving the lives of rural people, this will relieve pressure on urban areas while defusing the tension generated by large-scale rural-to-urban migration. More digitally based transfer systems have been set up in other parts of the world, including Flutterwave in Africa.

Tech literally brings the city to the countryside in the form of money transfers, and figuratively in terms of other services now available via cell phones.

Government Can Unleash Tech Innovation

Some enterprises developing or deploying such technology are for-profit, some are non-profits sponsored by donations, and some are hybrids, integrating a social cause into their for-profit structure. I believe that we should do all we can to support these efforts. We can support them personally, and encourage corporations and government to do the same. In addition to direct support, government can create a favorable tax environment and/or regulatory environment – this gives the market the incentive to support socially positive, fear-reducing technology.

Government can take a step further by partnering with the private sector to encourage innovation. For example, Fundación Chile, a non-profit corporation created in 1976 as a partnership between the government of Chile and BHP Billiton – Minera Escondida, was charged with introducing high-impact innovations in Chile. The organization's most notable success was introducing salmon farming to Chile, which lacks a native salmon population. Chile is now the second-largest salmon producer in the world. Furthermore, public – private partnerships focused on tech-enabled solutions can be used to address health, education, water, agriculture, finance, insurance and other issues affecting poor people.

We can also encourage cooperation between countries that have technology and those that have needs. A great example of this is the India-Israel Industrial R&D and Technological Innovation Fund, established in 2018. The beauty of this venture is that it allows an emerging market to leverage the technology and expertise of a First-World country to produce commercial solutions in various areas, including health, agriculture, energy, water, and information and communication technologies. For India this is an opportunity to find localized solutions to pressing problems, while for the Israeli companies involved, it is a chance to see if their solutions can become commercial on a large scale in a new market. As *Entrepreneur India*[25] points out, "Israel has over 400 companies offering AgriTech solutions. Indian start-ups that have a know-how of the market and local challenges can adopt these technologies to solve problems."

Re-Thinking Investment Funds

To support start-ups focusing on developing technology that addresses poverty and other pressing issues, we can rethink the way that large pools of money, often from investment funds, can be used. My friend Stephan Morais is the former Executive Director of Caixa Capital in Portugal, with 700 million Euros under management, where he led Technology Venture Capital and co-led Private Equity. He pointed out that the current structure of major investment funds gives them little incentive to open their wallets to small firms and entrepreneurs working to develop new ways to reduce lack. The typical venture capital investment fund is designed to operate for ten years, might invest in only twenty or thirty opportunities, and must return a healthy profit to its investors. This means that all of the fund's money must be invested within the first several years, and only in companies that seem very likely to produce large returns. Thus, the companies selected must be obviously commercially sustainable and have the ability to scale up across several geographies. Not all of the firms invested in will succeed, but the goal is to find at least a few that do fabulously well and can each be sold for many hundreds of millions of dollars – or more.

The investment funds are structured this way because the investors demand a good return within a decade, to compensate for the risk. Even if a fund manager had an interest in impact investing,

---

25 Sanchita Dash. "Indian-Israeli Start-ups as Partners is a Match Made in Heaven." Entrepreneur India, January 16, 2018. Accessible at https://www. entrepreneur.com/article/307543. Viewed May 11, 2018.

she or he can only do so if there is the prospect of a huge financial return.

Stephan Morais suggests that we can address this limitation by encouraging the development of a new funding model for this nascent asset class. Some investment funds could be set up with a longer time range, perhaps fifteen or twenty years, and have a mandate to consider a mixture of tech, commercial and social criteria. This structure would allow such funds to invest, at least partially, on the basis of principles for responsible investing.

In my view, in order for this approach to work, the new funding model would likely draw on a mix of philanthropic and corporate social investment funds, for these investors will be more willing to forgo some profit in the name of doing good while the asset class is being proven. This approach would balance the need for profit with the need to address problems facing emerging markets and people at the base of the pyramid, no matter where they may be, using tech-enabled solutions. Investors in the fund would understand and support the mandate, and would not pressure the fund manager to shift the focus to larger and more immediate profit. We must also remember that while these funds measure their financial and social impact, the measurement of the social impact should not be so onerous that dynamic companies are forced to spend more time measuring their impact than actually having an impact.

In addition, we can encourage tech corporations that currently do not have tech-enabled impact investment funds to set aside such money – at present, powerful new technologies are mainly applied to solve problems for other large businesses, or with the middle- to upper-class retail market in mind.

Fortunately, much of the technology we're speaking about is quite scalable, and globally so, as alluded to earlier, thanks to cellular telephones that can reach hundreds of millions of previously unreachable people, who are also potential customers. All across emerging markets there are common issues regarding health, education, agriculture, water, and more. Once a solution is found in one region of the world, it can be scaled to other parts of the world. This makes many of the new technologies we've been discussing potentially quite profitable and thus attractive to investors.

There are two cautionary notes. First, we must encourage those who support, develop, and deploy technology to remember that technology serves us best when it respects the humanity of all, and enables people and groups of all stripes to make common cause. No matter what the technology is designed to do, it should bring us together rather than elevate one group above another. Otherwise, it may increase group strife and widen the divide between the rich and the poor, which can only lead to class warfare and disaster. Second, we need to increase internet coverage in rural areas.

Diversity Encourages New Ideas

A number of new technological solutions have been developed by teams of diverse individuals.

This form of diversity is the practical application of the "Medici Effect," which was described in a 2004 book titled *The Medici Effect*, by Frans Johansson. The Medici were a Florentine family that played an important role in the Italian Renaissance. A fabulously wealthy banking dynasty, the Medici supported painters, sculptors, poets, architects, and philosophers during much of the 15th century. Lorenzo de' Medici's Humanist Academy drew together intellectuals and artists, including Leonardo da Vinci and Michelangelo, and encouraged the sharing of ideas. From this mix of ideas came tremendous advances in the arts and philosophy which helped propel the Italian Renaissance and influence us to this day.

The book argues that bringing together people from different cultures, educational backgrounds, industries and other factors produces true innovation. This is because people of differing backgrounds bring together diverse networks, realize there are multiple perspectives, are not fixated on a particular view and tend to make unusual associations. Diversity is indeed key to innovation and creativity, for the mixture of ideas and insights from different cultures, educational disciplines, industries, genders and generations, encourages people to see things in new ways and develop new solutions.

A number of studies have looked at the benefits of diversity, including adding women to formerly all-male teams, and minorities to previously all-white teams. One such study found that when women are added to previously all-male leadership teams in firms whose strategy is based on innovation, the firm's performance improves.[26] Other forms of diversity are also beneficial, as studies have shown that when people of different races, political affiliations, and other markers of difference are brought together, they tend to work harder to prepare better, listen to each other more carefully, and treat contributions from racial or opinion minorities as novel information.

You need not have a laboratory or field study setting to be innovative, for any time you bring together a diverse group of people, ideas can begin to cross-pollinate. Even in something as simple and informal as a break room or book reading club, the results can be transformative. And, of course, encouraging people to mix can break down old conceptions of "us" and "them," with positive effects that can ripple across society.

Promoting Diversity, Mixing Private & Public
My friend Earl Valencia co-created a start-up accelerator and fund in the Philippines that prizes diversity *and* uses a mix of private and public know-how, making it an intriguing model for other start-up accelerators and investment funds.

Born and raised in the Philippines, Earl earned advanced degrees from Cornell University and the Stanford Graduate School of Business. He started working as an aerospace engineer in the U.S. and then moved to Silicon Valley – which is when the CEO of a Hong Kong-based private equity firm called First Pacific asked him what he really wanted to be doing later in life.

Right away Earl knew the answer: He wanted to return to the

---

26 Dezsö, Cristian L. and Ross, David Gaddis, Does Female Representation in Top Management Improve Firm Performance? A Panel Data Investigation (March 9, 2011). Robert H. Smith School Research Paper No. RHS 06-104. Available at SSRN: https://ssrn.com/abstract=1088182.

Philippines to invest in science and tech ideas that have great potential, but that would be passed over by investors because "the names were wrong." In the Philippines and other emerging markets your name is, to a large degree, your destiny, for people pay close attention to your family name and background when deciding whether to invest in, or work with, you.

With the backing of this CEO and First Pacific, Earl co-founded IdeaSpace, a start-up accelerator and fund "designed for diversity." Teams from all over the Philippines were invited to submit applications, and the applicants' names and schools/universities attended were removed from the paperwork before the ideas were judged. Removing the names of the applicants and their schools, and all the associations they carried with them, produced instant diversity: 40 percent of the company founders IdeaSpace has invested in are female, a tremendous increase in gender diversity. And a great many of the founders came from outside the greater Manila area, the usual source of applications. Right from the start, Earl was supporting gender- and geographically diverse start-ups, pulling in talent and ideas that traditionally would have been totally ignored – and *were* being overlooked, right up to the moment he decided to design for diversity.

One of the start-ups IdeaSpace funded, called Coins.ph, had an Israeli founder, a Chief Technology Officer from Scandinavia, and a Filipino Design Officer. Another, called SALt (Sustainable Alternative Lighting), which produces a "sustainable and cost effective ecologically designed lantern activated by salt water," is led by a female professor.

According to Earl, "it's all about meritocracy, giving people the best chance to succeed. How do I level the playing field so that people with the 'wrong name' or who attended the 'wrong school' or come from the 'wrong place' get access to investment funds and other forms of assistance? How do we hack the existing system so that people have a chance to succeed, regardless of who they are and where they're from?"

In addition to diversity, IdeaSpace deliberately mixed philanthropic funds with private equity investing discipline, and the private and public sectors.

First Pacific allocated twelve-and-a-half million dollars to IdeaSpace, but did not treat this money as a financial investment. Instead, it looked upon it as a philanthropic fund to be applied on a commercial, private equity basis. That is, not money to be donated, deducted from taxes and then forgotten, but rather as money to be invested in science and tech ideas that could benefit the country *and* earn a profit.

Although founded by people from the world of private equity, IdeaSpace sought out the best from both the private and public sectors. It quickly developed ties with the ministries of trade, science, and information technology in the Philippines. This gives the start-ups supported by IdeaSpace the opportunity to be show-cased, acquire knowledge, attract talent, and possibly secure business from the public sector. At the same time, IdeaSpace invited corporate executives and venture capitalists from all over the world to participate in judging the start-ups applying for support, and then had execs and subject experts serve as mentors or board members to the start-ups. In addition to expertise, this brings perspectives from all over the world to these Filipino start-ups. IdeaSpace also established ties with highly rated American universities: Harvard, Stanford and MIT. Students from these universities serve as interns with the start-ups, bringing with them technical know-how and new perspectives. When their internships are over, they return home with new insights of their own, which could only have been developed by stepping away.

First Pacific, which owns a number of large businesses, also grants a six-month "entrepreneur sabbatical" to any of its employees who apply for and receive support from IdeaSpace. This allows people who have intriguing ideas, but for various reasons cannot take the risk of leaving their jobs, the chance to become innovators and entrepreneurs. Some of them succeed, while those who return to their corporate jobs do so enriched, for during their six-months they earned a "mini MBA," learning to think like owners rather than employees. Bringing this new mindset back to the corporate world makes them better employees.

In addition to promoting diversity, infusing philanthropic funds with private sector discipline, mixing the corporate world with the public sector, drawing in talent to the Philippines and "exporting" Filipino talent and perspective to the rest of the world, IdeaSpace is also fiercely committed to the idea of creating the next generation of entrepreneurs with country-building ideas. The way this works is quite simple. Even if a chosen start-up's founders hail from outside the Philippines, the company sets up in the Philippines and hires locally. The early hires work for a company with global aspirations, watching and learning as it scales up. In years to come, some of these early employees will take this invaluable knowledge with them as they create their own companies.

Earl is dedicated to promoting diversity on various levels, perhaps because of his life experiences. He experienced socioeconomic diversity in his early years of university in the Philippines, where he attended public university with the children of farmers and taxi drivers. This was a highly rated and very selective university, only accepting the very top tier students. Sharing class with students from the lower economic strata made him aware of the talent that was routinely overlooked. Transferring to universities in the United States, he mixed with the sons and daughters of the elite, as well as the children of less financially endowed families who demonstrated their academic talent in the classroom and on admission tests. His career was diverse. Working in the Silicon Valley introduced him to different business models; working as an aerospace engineer gave him an idea of what is possible from a science and research perspective; and interacting with people from different backgrounds introduced him to new perspectives. By "designing for diversity" in IdeaSpace, he is introducing the benefits of diversity to more and more people.

Conclusion

The waves of new technology pouring out of innovators' minds can help address many of the lacks the world faces. At the moment, sadly, much of this technological innovation is designed to address the needs of the wealthy and middle class, as well as those of large corporations. If we can turn more and more of this innovation to address the needs of the poor and marginalized, we will reduce a great deal of the lack that drives fear, and the fear that has driven history for so long.

Jesmane Boggenpoel is an experienced business executive and a former Head of Business Engagement for Africa at the World Economic Forum in Switzerland. She has served on the boards of various South African and international organizations. She is a Chartered Accountant (South Africa) and holds a Master's degree from Harvard University's JFK School of Government. Jesmane was honored as a Young Global Leader of the World Economic Forum and is a Harvard Mason fellow.

9 781928 455288